INTRODUCTION

Hi, I'm Allison. Feel free to call me Allie. Everyone does.

Let me show you around this book.

This book is your toolbox for teaching your child at home. I created the activities with parents as teachers in mind. I give basic instructions not because I don't think you would understand my long-winded explanations about specific skill development, but because I know you are busy. You need an idea that you know will work and your child will benefit from. That's what I have filled this book with.

Feel free to email me at allie@notimeforflashcards.com if you want any of those long-winded explanations; I'm happy to bore you with them.

Oh, and I know you don't have the huge supply closet I have at preschool, so these activities use everyday materials.

Allison McDonald, B.A, B.Ed, M.S

HOW TO USE THIS BOOK

TAKE A DEEP BREATH

You never thought you'd be homeschooling your kids, did you? Does it feel impossible? It's not. **You can do this.** You don't need a huge budget to spend on materials. You don't need a graduate degree in early childhood education (don't worry, I have one, and I've got your back), and you don't need to set aside hours to plan and implement these activities. Start small, be consistent, and don't forget to breathe.

THIS ISN'T PRESCHOOL

This is not a book that will replace preschool exactly. Whatever your reasons are for homeschooling, this book will help you do just that. This book is filled with activities that busy parents can use to keep their children learning, no matter how busy they are. This is not a complete curriculum with scope and sequence. It's more like a great big buffet of excellent choices to pick and choose from daily. Try to choose something from a few sections every day and take note of how to make it easier or harder to meet your child's needs.

FOCUS ON CONNECTION

The activities in this book are beneficial, and they are vital for creating a strong foundation for future learning. However, they are not more important than feeling loved, feeling safe, and feeling calm. If you only have 10 minutes to spend with your preschooler, spend it playing if you have a little more cuddle up with a book after you play. If you still have more, grab this book and do an activity or two each day. Before children can learn anything, they need to know they are safe and loved.

HOW TO USE THIS BOOK

EVERYDAY MATERIALS

You don't need all the fancy classroom materials your child's preschool teacher has. Letter magnets can be replaced with pieces of paper with letters written on them. Fancy paint can be replaced with .99 cent watercolors, and climbing a tree is arguably more beneficial than the playground equipment anyway. All of these activities use everyday materials. In the appendix, you will find a basic supply list, book list, sight words lists, nursery rhymes, fingerplays, song lyrics, and my favorite playdough recipe.

MAKE IT ROUTINE

If this is just a short-term homeschooling gig, you don't need to set aside a schoolroom in your home or make a strict daily schedule. If you are planning on homeschooling long-term, go for it, you do you! However, you should have a predictable routine. Even it's just that every day during your work-at-home lunch break, you and your child do one activity and then read at bedtime. Or maybe you can spend 30 minutes every day when your workday is done completing two activities, great! You don't have to set the alarm, so it's the exact same time every day. It just has to be predictable.

VARIETY AND REPETITION

I know I just said to make it predictable, but now I am telling you to shake things up. Specifically, try to rotate activities from different areas of learning (math, literacy, fine motor, art) to create a balanced experience for your child. Now to contradict myself AGAIN, repetition is your friend. Repeating activities is expected and encouraged. Revisit favorites, revisit fun but challenging ones until they aren't challenging, and know that repetition isn't usually dull for kids. It provides security. That's why they love reading that terrible picture book you hate every night. Yes, you should suck it up and read it for the 300th time.

PLAN YOUR WEEK

Some days will be perfect. Most won't. It's ok. Even veteran teachers have terrible days. Take a few minutes on the weekend to plan. Keep it simple and you'll make this a habit.

ACTIVITY:	MATERIALS:
BEDTIME BOOK:	

ACTIVITY:	MATERIALS:
BEDTIME BOOK:	

ACTIVITY:	MATERIALS:
BEDTIME BOOK:	

ACTIVITY:	MATERIALS:
BEDTIME BOOK:	

ACTIVITY:	MATERIALS:
BEDTIME BOOK:	

CONTENTS

ACTIVITIES

EVERYDAY LESSONS
LITERACY
MATH
SCIENCE
SENSORY PLAY
ART EXPLORATIONS
FINE MOTOR
GROSS MOTOR
SOCIAL-EMOTIONAL
BEDTIME READING

APPENDIX

PRESCHOOL BOOK LIST
BASIC SUPPLY LIST
PLAYDOUGH RECIPE
SIGHT WORDS LIST
LINKS TO FREE PRINTABLE RESOURCES
SONGS AND FINGERPLAYS
NURSERY RHYMES

EVERYDAY LESSONS
ANTI-BIAS AND ANTI-RACISM RESOURCES

Teaching your children about the diverse world around them in their community and family is crucial. Learning about their own culture, as well as cultures different from their own, is vital. Learning about race and racism is a must. However, these lessons aren't quick or super simple, which is the mission of this book, so I don't have quick lessons with cute pictures for these topics.

Instead, I encourage you to read books with all kinds of characters with your children, some with families just like yours, some with families, nothing like yours. I encourage you to make food that is significant to your culture and foods from other cultures with your child when you have enough time in your schedule to dive into a new recipe. Listen to music in another language and expose your child to diverse arts when possible.

In my classroom, I use an emergent curriculum, which means that as my students show interest, make comments, have conflict, or notice something new, I adjust and teach these "emerging" ideas. This is where most of my teachable moments about justice, injustice, and bias come from. I encourage you to jump on these teachable moments with your children too. I encourage you to read books about racism and injustice and use the bedtime reading questions to dive into these topics at the level your child is ready for; psst! They are smart little humans, and if we offer them a chance to talk about big tough topics, they usually blow us away with their insights.

EVERYDAY LESSONS
ANTI-BIAS AND ANTI-RACISM RESOURCES

Here are some fantastic resources you can use as you dive into this essential part of educating your child at home:

Here Wee Read – https://www.instagram.com/hereweeread/
An excellent account filled with diverse books, discussions about inclusion, and so much more.

The Conscious Kid - theconsciouskid.org Parenting and Education through a Critical Race Lens

How To Teach Kids About Race and Racism -
https://www.pbs.org/parents/talking-about-racism
PBS Parents

We Need Diverse Books - https://diversebooks.org
A site committed to diverse books.

Embrace Race - https://www.embracerace.org/
Resources for raising the next generation to be anti-racist

Teaching Tolerance - Equity and Diversity. - https://www.tolerance.org
This is a teaching resource but filled with wonderful ideas, lessons, and resources.

No Time For Flash Cards- https://www.notimeforflashcards.com/category/diverse-books
Diverse Picture Book Lists

LITERACY ACTIVITIES

Literacy is more than learning to read. It's speaking, writing, listening, and singing too.

LITERACY ACTIVITIES

LISTEN TO THE BEAT

Listening is a huge part of literacy foundations and if we expect our children to learn all the letter sounds and to be able to discriminate between them, we need to work on listening skills in general!

Clap out a beat using your hands and then ask your child to stamp it out with their feet. Now stomp out a beat with your feet and ask them to repeat it by clapping.

You can add counting to this too - the goal is for your child to listen carefully and be able to replicate it.

I'M GOING ON A TRIP AND TAKING...

Before kiddos attach what a letter looks like or its name to words, we need them to hear letter sounds and identify similar ones. You can do that so easily at home with only a tiny bit of prep. This game is make-believe, so pretend you are going on a trip somewhere awesome but the only rule is you can only pack things that start with the same sound.

For example - I'm going on a trip to Canada and taking cookies, cake, candles, and cans.

It doesn't have to be sensical at all and *spelling/ letter matching isn't part of this lesson, it is all about sounds.* So if you are going to Canada you could also take kites or kyaks.

GOOFY GILBERT GOES TOO SLOW

This syllable blending activity is adapted from a suggestion from the book Speech to Print by Louisa Cook Moats, which is a wonderful read if you are a grad student but not such a great bedtime read for most parents. I am so excited to do this activity with my Prek students, I had to add it to this updated version of Everyday Preschool.

Grab a stuffed animal or puppet and pretend that they talk TOO slowly. "Oh, man Gilbert talks too slowly. Can you listen to what Gilbert is saying and say it faster?" Now say 2 syllable letters slowly breaking up the syllables.

"Tooth....brush...." kids --> yell out toothbrush!
"ba...con" kids--> yell out bacon!

If they have mastered two syllables, start blending with three.

LITERACY ACTIVITIES

FAMILY NAME CLAP

Clap out the syllables in your family names and help your child learn that words are made up of specific sounds. Explain that words and names are made up of chunks of sounds. Then clap them out. This skill of segmenting syllables is a basic literacy skill that comes well before most others, even though many skip right over it.

Al (clap) - i (clap)- son (clap) - 3!

Cathe (clap) - rine(clap) - 2!

Make it easier -> This activity is pretty simple to start with, but you can keep it shorter, focusing on only a few names.

Make it harder -> Make a list of family members' names and write how many syllables they have next to their name.

SILLY RHYMES ALL THE TIMES

Nonsense words are a great way to work on rhyming, and you can do this activity anywhere. Explain to your child that you will make up your own words, but the only rule is that they need to rhyme. Give them a few examples of some nonsense rhymes to get them started.

Now yell out a word - it can be real or nonsense and help them brainstorm a nonsense rhyme to match it. After they find the rhyme, now ask them what this word means.

Make it easier -> Ask your child to call out words, and you think up the rhyme they will still be learning with your modeling.

Make it harder -> Choose a few of your created words and write them out on a sheet of paper and their invented definitions.

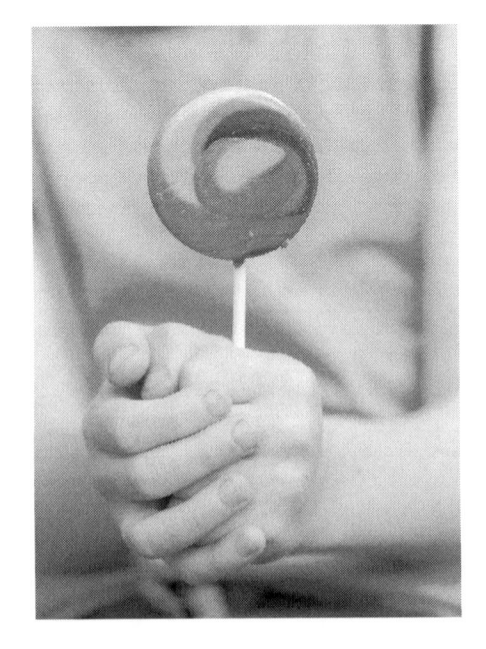

LAMP, LION, LOLLIPOP!

This game builds on the sound discrimination skills that "Going on trip... introduced. Now it's more concrete with toys.

Dig through your child's toybox and fid toys that start with the same sound. Aim for at least three toys or other household items for each sound. Pop them all in a pile or basket. Now pick one out and ask your child to find the others that start with that sound.

Make it easier –> stick to matching up pairs of sounds instead of groups.

Make it harder –> If your child is ready for attaching the letters to the sounds, instead of pulling out a toy, say, " Find all the toys that start with the sound the letter L makes." Remember that letters can make multiple sounds and this about sounds not spelling so knife and nest are a perfectly acceptable pair.

LITERACY ACTIVITIES

SHAVING CREAM LETTERS

You will need some shaving cream and a cookie sheet or other smooth surfaces like a tray for this sensory literacy activity. Spread some shaving cream on the tray or sheet evenly.

Show your child how you can use your finger to write letters with it. Start with the letters of their name, writing both the upper and lowercase versions of these letters. Between letters, you can "erase" by spreading the shaving cream smoothly over the surface.

Make it easier -> Stick to your child's first initial. Write the letter in its uppercase form and have your child trace it with their finger. Now try the lowercase.

Make it harder -> Make or write sight words instead of letters.

HIGHLIGHTER LETTER HUNT

Time to use junk mail for good. Grab a highlighter and some junk mail to practice letter recognition and visual discrimination skills. Choose a letter or two to hunt for in the junk mail. When your child finds it use the highlighter to mark it.

Make it easier -> instead of specific letters, ask your child to highlight the letters they like, as they do label the letters for them. "You just highlighted the letter r."

Make it harder -> Scan the flyer and find simple words like and, to, and the. Write them out on scrap paper and ask your child to find and highlight them when they do.

TWINKLE TWINKLE LITTLE STAR

Nursery rhymes are such an essential tool for early literacy. Recite this classic with your child and then illustrate it together. Grab some crayons and plain paper and draw a picture of the little star together. If your child enjoys this activity, try it again with other nursery rhymes.

Make it easier -> This one is pretty simple as is.

Make it harder -> After drawing the picture, find a spot on the paper to write the nursery rhyme. Have your child recite it as you write it out. This simple step helps to cement the idea that spoken words translate into text.

LITERACY ACTIVITIES

MUSICAL LETTERS

Get some plain paper and write letters on them. If you have painter's tape, you can make the letters right on your floor. Use a mix of letters, but there is no need to use all twenty-six. Place them around a room with the furniture pushed aside, so there is room to move and groove when the music plays. Play the music and groove. Pause the music and CALL out a letter. Your child should stand on that letter. Repeat!

Make it easier -> Use only a few letters and make them all different colors. When it's time to call out the letter, call it out as" RED H" or "BLUE T" whatever colors the letters are. This scaffold gives your child help to find the letters since they have the color as a hint.

Make it harder -> Make or write sight words instead of letters.

NAME PUZZLES

Write your child's name on a piece of paper. Use an uppercase letter for the first letter and lowercase for the remaining letters. Cut the letters out, so each letter is its own strip of paper. Pop them in an envelope. Present the envelope to your child saying, " What is in here? Let's find out!" Take each letter out of the envelope and have your child name it if they can. If not, you name it. " Look, it's a lowercase l. What's next? Oh, look lowercase i until you get all the letters out. They do not have to be in order. When they are all out, ask your child if they recognize the letters. "What do you think these letters could spell?" Let your child play with them. Together spell your child's name. Mix them up and spell it again.

Make it easier -> Write out their name on the 2nd piece of paper and have them place the letters on top, matching them to the intact name.

BOOK LETTER HUNT

Write out the alphabet on a piece of paper. Sit down with a familiar book. You won't be reading it, just using it to find letters. Look for each letter, turn the page from time to time for a new search area.

Make it easier -> Instead of the whole alphabet, look only for 5-10 letters.

Make it harder -> Look for simple sight words instead of letters.

LITERACY ACTIVITIES

COLOR SORTING LETTERS

You don't need magnetic letters for this activity, but if you have them, it will save you some time. If you do not have magnetic letters grab some white paper and at least three different color markers. Use the markers to make letters on the paper in 3 or more colors. Cut them out into small cards with one letter on each. Mix. Invite your child to help you sort the letters by color. Label letters for your child as they do. "Look a blue m!"

Make it easier -Use the same letters over and over-focus on only 3 or 4 different letters.

Make it harder -> Write out simple 2-3 letter sight words all in the same color. Cut into individual letters. After sorting by color, build sight words with the sorted letters. Find sight word lists in the appendix.

WRITING CENTER

Writing centers sound fancy and expensive. They aren't, and they don't have to take up a bunch of space either. All you need are some fun writing tools, paper, and minimal extras. Pop it on a tray, in a small reusable container, or even a Ziploc to store it. Now and then, bring it out and invite your child to create something.

Make it easier -> Start with the basics; stick to paper and crayons.

Make it harder -> Add in some index cards with family names so your child can write notes to family, fancy pens or smelly markers, and letter stickers!

HOST A PODCAST

Not a real podcast, just one you record and listen to. This is a fun a deceptively simple activity. You might want to find a great kid-friendly podcast to listen to before doing this with your child. "Wow in the World" by NPR is my favorite. After listening, ask your child if they want to make a podcast just for your family. Use your voice recorder on your smartphone and have a chat! The goal for this activity is to work on oral language and for your child to get a chance to hear themselves speak too.

Make it easier -> Skip the recording and play podcast with a "microphone," which can be a spatula from your kitchen.

Make it harder -> If your child can read, write a basic script together before recording.

LITERACY ACTIVITIES

FISHING FOR LETTERS

Get 4-5 pieces of paper. Draw some basic fish, write a letter on each fish. Cut out. Make a "pond" with a tray, blanket, or use the floor. Pop the fish face down in the pond. Invite your child to go fishing. As they get a fish, ask them to tell you what they got. " Yes, that's a lowercase r!"

Make it easier -> Limit the number of fish to only 5-10, use letters your child is familiar with like the letters in their name.

Make it harder -> Use sight words or names to fish for instead.

WRITE A LETTER

Gather some writing materials – use what you have! Sit down together a write a letter to someone you miss. After writing, have your child draw a picture for the recipient too. Address and stamp the envelope and walk it to the mailbox.

Make it easier -> Have your child dictate the letter to you.

Make it harder -> Have your child write the letter and guide them by addressing the envelope.

PLAYDOUGH LETTERS

Time for some playdough! Using the dough form some letters, starting with your child's first initial. Can your child make their first initial? What about the same letter, but in its lowercase form? Try together. If you have letter stamps or cookie cutters, get them and add them in for more fun!

Make it easier -> Make X's and Os rolling out the playdough is beneficial all on its own, don't fret if they aren't ready to make letters.

Make it harder -> Make or write sight words in the playdough with letter stamps or form the letters. Don't forget we have sight word lists in our appendix.

LITERACY ACTIVITIES

ANIMAL SYLLABLE STOMP

Stomp out the syllables in animal names and learn more about what makes words. As noted in the family name activity a few pages ago, segmenting syllables is a foundational literacy skill. This skill is important because once children are ready to decode words (sound words out), they need to break them down into sounds (segmentation). This is a fun way to work on that skill.

Yell out an animal and together stomp out the syllables.

El (stomp)-le (stomp)-phant (stomp)

Make it easier -> Limit the number of animals to only 5-6

Make it harder -> Stomp out a dozen or more animals. Just make sure no downstairs neighbors are home!

MAKE YOUR OWN MAP

Writing on a vertical surface is hugely beneficial to writing development. So I'm here to ask you to take some time to do that, and a fun way is to make a wall map.

If you have a wall-mounted chalkboard, you are set. If not, pop some paper on your wall with painter's tape. Give them some writing utensils and tell them this is their map to create their own land! Next, title it with your child's name and land after that - so if your child's name is Owen, title the map "Owenland."

Make it easier -> Use a smaller piece of paper so that the task doesn't overwhelm your child.

Make it harder -> Look at maps together and notice the elements they have, like legends. Incorporate these elements into your wall map.

WRITE A RECIPE

Grab a cookbook and look through it. Show your child the ingredients list and the text that includes the instructions for making the recipe. Tell them that today they get to create their own recipe. It can be for real food or something silly like a recipe for a rainbow unicorn! Write it out together. Encourage your child to do as much of the writing as possible. If not, have them draw some of the steps for the recipe.

Make it easier -> Have your child dictate the recipe to you, and you do the writing.

Make it harder -> Read other recipes together and make something to eat!

LITERACY ACTIVITIES

FAMILY SING ALONG

Singing is an important early literacy activity. Children can play with words, rhymes, and even develop new vocabulary.
Choose 2-3 fun action songs from the appendix and have a little sing-along.

Make it easier -> This activity is pretty simple to start with, but you can keep it shorter, focusing on only 1-2 songs.

Make it harder -> After singing, have your child draw a picture of their favorite part of their favorite song.

FAMILY PHOTO STORYTELLING

Get snuggly and scroll through those photos on your phone together. Ask your child to tell you about different images that are likely to get them talking. Special events, birthday parties, and family trips all make great stories. This is a great time to talk about the things and people we miss being at home. Kids are perceptive, and ignoring the elephant in the room doesn't protect them, acknowledging their feelings does.

Make it easier -> Make a small album with specific photos the night before and limit the activity to that handful of photos. A must if you are strapped for time.

Make it harder -> Print out a few photos leaving space on the paper to write. Ask your child to write about the pictures or have them dictate what they would like to write and write it for them.

I SPY LETTER SOUNDS

This is a game I played with my children in waiting rooms, on airplanes, in the grocery checkout line. It's so simple. Look around and find an object in the room. Say, "I spy with my little eye something that starts with the sound "mm" "Yes, microwave! It starts with the sound mm." Try not to drag the letter sounds out too much; make it quick. Repeat the sound if needed instead of dragging them out.

Make it easier –> Search for sounds for a few minutes and then switch it up for colors or shapes.

Make it harder –> Try searching for rhymes instead " I spy with my little eye, something that rhymes with pear. Yes, chair!"

LITERACY ACTIVITIES

SIMON SAYS SIT

Understanding position words like above, below, behind, etc. isn't only about vocabulary; it is also about understanding and communicating with others effectively. This game is always a hit. Sit on a couch with your child. Tell them that you will be playing a game called Simon says, explain the rules if they aren't familiar. Remind them that they only move if you call out Simon says before the command when they are ready call out commands using positional words. "Simon says, sit next to me." "Simon says, sit under the table." "Simon says, sit behind me."

Make it easier -> Focus on 1-2 positional words like under, next to, or in front.

Make it harder -> Go faster! This game can be delightful with kids who have mastered these positional words.

PARTS OF A BOOK

For this activity, you will need a big picture book, a pen, and some post-its. Ask your child if they know the names of all the parts of a book. Point to the title and ask your child what it is. If they say it's the book's name, say something. "Yes, we call that a title." Write "title" down on a post-it and ask your child to pop it on the title. Continue with parts like the cover, author, illustrator, spine, table of contents if you have one, page numbers, etc. you should have a bunch of post-its on the book by the time you are done.

Make it easier -> Focus on the basics, like title, author, illustrator, and cover.

Make it harder -> Ask your child to show you how a book works. Tell them that you will pretend to be from outer space and need your child to explain books to you since you've never seen one before.

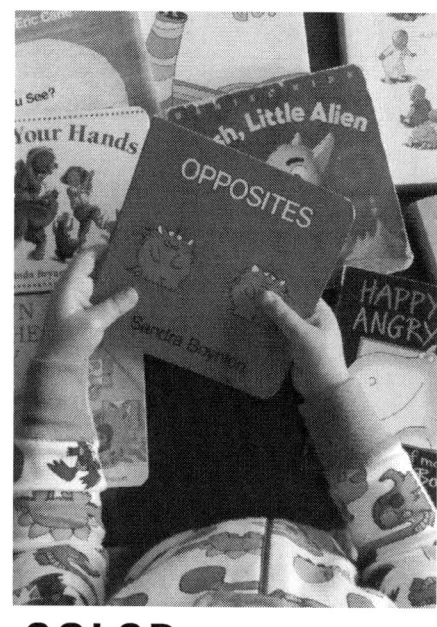

LETTER SEARCH & COLOR

All you need for this activity is a piece of paper, some markers, and a pen. Write a bunch of letters on the paper. Leave some space at the bottom of the paper. Do not worry about getting every letter on the paper; try to make sure you have included some familiar letters like the letters in your child's name. In the space you left at the bottom of the paper, choose a few letters from the bunch, write them in this space with a squiggle of color next to it. These will be the letters your child is searching for and the color they need to color it when they do.

Make it easier –> Use fewer letters and keep the number of letters to search for low too. Search together.

Make it harder –> Instead of color by letter, try sight words instead. A list of sight words can be found in the appendix.

LITERACY ACTIVITIES

WINDOW WASHER

I love this activity because it's so easy to change as your child's skills develop. Grab a dry erase marker and write some letters on your window. Hand your child a cloth and call out letters.

Make it easier -> Focus on 2-3 letters and have multiple copies of them on the window. This helps your child feel successful and reinforces their abilities.

Make it harder -> Have upper and lowercase letters and specify each as you call them out.

LETTER DIG

You will need a cookie sheet, a paintbrush, some rice, and magnetic letters for this activity. If you don't have magnetic letters, you can use letters written on paper. Place the letters on the cookie sheet and cover them with rice. Hand your child the paintbrush and tell them that they are letter "archeologists" looking for ancient letters. They must carefully dig with the paintbrush moving the rice away from the precious letters. They should call the letter name out when they find the letter. Keep going!

Make it easier -> Use mostly letters your child is familiar with, only one or two more challenging ones. Label those for them.

Make it harder -> Ask your child to suggest a word that starts with that letter sound when they uncover the letter.

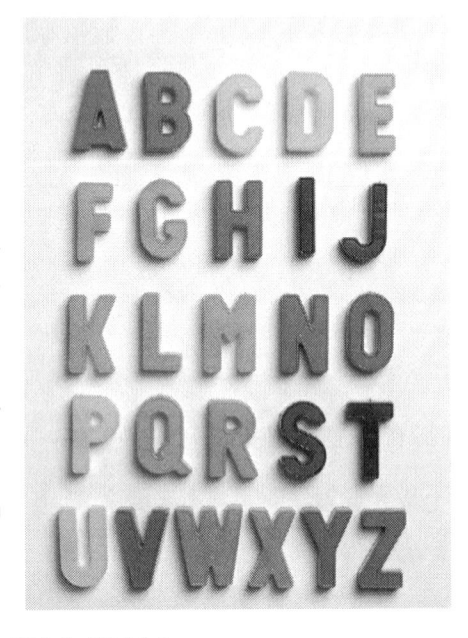

ALPHABET SENSORY BIN

Create an inviting alphabet sensory bin with items you already have at home. Letter magnets, foam letters, letter cookie cutters, letter beads... whatever you have or can find at the dollar store are great options. Add some dried beans (don't use dry kidney beans. They are toxic) and some scoops and tongs. Explore with your child, "Hey, look, it's an uppercase W!" keep digging and scooping. Follow your child's lead and have fun.

Make it easier –> You can't really have fun and play!

Make it harder –> Make sure you have all the letters in your child's name and challenge them to find and spell their name.

LITERACY ACTIVITIES

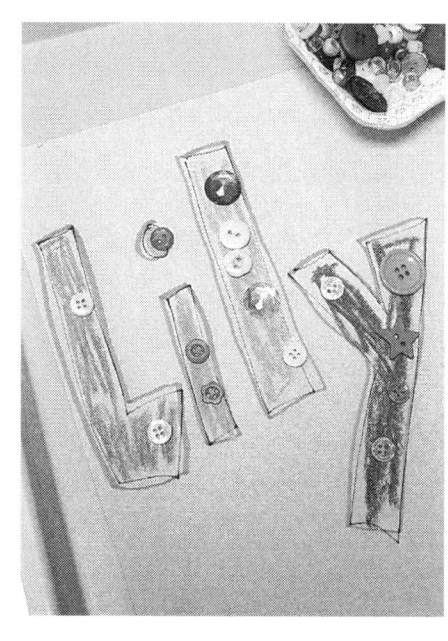

NAME SIGN

Learning to recognize and spell your name is an essential step for developing literacy. Not only do children see these letters often, but they are also meaningful. Use your child's name to start learning about letters, spelling, and as a source of pride. You can use whatever you have. Paper and crayons. Construction paper and plastic jewels, markers, and glitter glue. Search and find what you have and use it to make this meaningful sign.

Make it easier -> Have your child decorate just their first initial. This is what we call "Your letter" in my preschool classroom, and it's a great starting point for letter recognition.

Make it harder -> Make bedroom signs for everyone in your family or make one for a friend and send it to them in the mail!

LETTER MATCH UP

Matching up lower and uppercase letters is an activity that helps children recognize letters but also learn that letters come in various sizes and serve different functions. You don't need fancy equipment for this activity. Grab a few sheets of plain paper, a marker, and scissors. Write a few uppercase letters on one sheet of paper. You can make it fancy if you want with colors, but you don't have to. Write lowercase letters on another sheet and cut them out so they are in little squares. Pop them in a small ziplock or a bowl. When you are ready to play, pull a lowercase letter out of the bag and match it to the uppercase letters on the other sheet of paper.

Make it easier -> Use fewer letters and use the same color marker for the same letter, giving your child a hint since they match.

Make it harder -> Try this with sight words instead. Find sight word lists in the appendix.

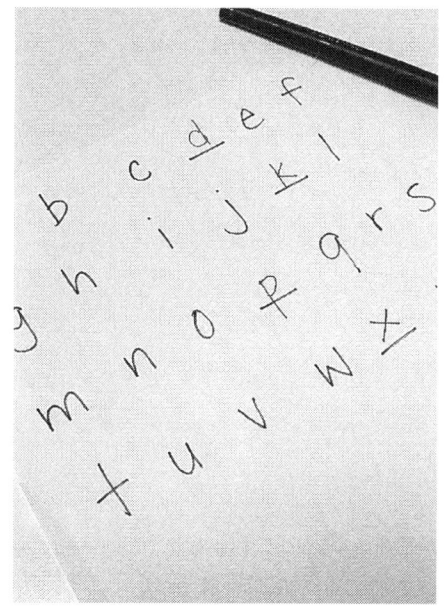

MISSING LETTERS

Get some paper and a marker. Write out the alphabet on paper leaving a few letters out. You can do upper or lowercase letters with this alphabet game. Explain to your child that some letters are missing, and you need their help to find them. Sing the alphabet song while touching each letter. When you get to a blank spot, stop and ask, "Wait, what goes here?" Use the alphabet song to figure it out. Go back to a and sing, pointing to each letter. Eventually, you will be pointing at the blank space, and the child will be saying the letter in the song. "You found the letter, yes, it's a g!" write the letter in and continue. Each time you get to a blank space, go back to a and sing to find the missing letter.

Make it easier -> Only leave out 2-3 letters.

Make it harder -> leave out 15+

LITERACY ACTIVITIES

WRITE A THANK YOU NOTE

Teaching your child to be grateful can seem abstract. How do you teach a 3-year-old to be thankful when they are naturally (and developmentally appropriately) so self-centered? With actions. Sit down and write simple thank you notes to people who matter to you. They don't have to be fancy. Write one to the delivery guy, or your mail carrier. Write one to a teacher or religious leader.

Make it easier -> Write the note on a post-it. The space is small and less intimidating. Or draw a picture instead.

Make it harder -> Write a postcard. You can also use this time to teach your kiddo about addressing mail properly.

ALPHABET SCAVENGER HUNT

Go on an adventure together, looking for things that start with each letter of the alphabet! You can write the alphabet own on a piece of scrap paper and check each letter off as you find things. A – apple, B – bed, C – cat, D – door, keep going!

Make it easier -> Search only for the letters in your child's name.

Make it harder -> Ditch the alphabet and use sight words. Find a list of sight words in the appendix. Write them on small pieces of paper and say the word, have your child find the word hidden around your home, or just scattered on a table.

RHYME AND FIND

Rhyming is my favorite way to play with words and sounds. This skill is crucial because it helps children learn how to break the sounds in words apart, which is vital for literacy development. Children don't know that's what they are doing at first and we don't have to explain that, just play.

This game is a little like I-spy, you choose an object in the room and tell your child that the object rhymes with; and say a rhyme. Then your child searches the room for the object.
For example, "The object rhymes with nook." <-- book.
"The object rhymes with bear." <-- chair.
The rhymes can be made up too. Bouch for couch, nable for table, etc. because the goal is to play with rhyming sounds.

Make it easier -> Use simple words like cup, hat, and ball.

MATH ACTIVITIES

Your home is filled with everyday math. Objects to count, shapes to find, and things to measure.

MATH ACTIVITIES

ROLL & COVER GAMES

This is a simple math game that works on many skills. All you need is a sheet of paper, a pencil, a die, and something to mark your places like buttons, coins, or even stickers. To make the game board draw dots on a paper. I usually make 3-4 rows of 6 dots. If you want to print out a colorful game board, I have five pre-made options on my website for free. The link is in the appendix.

Roll the die, count the dots, and cover that many dots on your game board with your markers.

Make it easier -> Put fewer dots on the game board or take turns rolling and covering. This is a great way to model how to play for younger kiddos.

Make it harder -> use two dice, adding the two numbers together to see how many dots you need to cover.

STUFFED ANIMAL LINE UP

Gather 5-10 of your child's stuffed animals and talk a little about how they look. Talk about their colors, their textures, which animals they are. Ask your child if they can help you line the toys up by size, starting with the smallest. Line them up by size, try to use words like longest, shortest, taller, and shorter. If your child isn't the stuffed animal aficionado that mine is, no worries you can use anything for this activity; shoes, books, socks...

Make it easier -> Use stuffed animals that are obviously different in lengths, use only 5.

Make it harder -> Use a measuring tape to measure and record each toy's height before placing them in the line.

SORT BY COLOR

Gather up a bunch of toys (nothing multicolored, each toy should be one color) – they can be big stuffed animals, little matchbox cars, Lego, etc. Use what you have. Place them in a big pile and tell your child that you need their help finding out how many toys of each color you have in the collection. After sorting every toy by color, count, and see which color is most prevalent in your toy box.

Make it easier -> Use fewer toys.

Make it harder -> After sorting by color sort by size.

MATH ACTIVITIES

NUMBER HUNT

Scavenger hunts are always fun. They are also a great way to make sure your child stays active, even if they are stuck inside. Use some post-it notes with numbers or just use paper, and hide them all over! Use at least ten and hide them around your home. Now it's time to go hunting! What numbers did you find? Label the numbers that your child doesn't recognize saying something like, "Where did you find this number 4?"

Make it easier -> Hunt together. Especially with children just starting to recognize numbers. As you help find the numbers, labeling them casually can be an excellent scaffold. "I see a two by the window!"

Make it harder –> Use a second set of post-it notes and line them up on your wall to make a number line. As your child finds a number, have them come and match it up to the number line.

KITCHEN COUNTING

Grab a piece of paper and title it "How many do we have?" then, write the names of the items you want to count together. Plate, spoons, kid cups, wine glasses, bowls. Whatever you have. After counting each item, write the number down, if your child can write or can't but wants to try, have them write it. Don't worry about how perfect the four does or doesn't look.

Make it easier -> Have a small group of kitchen items out to count, for example, three forks, two cups, and four spoons.

Make it harder –> before counting, ask your child to make a prediction about which items will have the most, how many do they think there are? After counting, make a simple bar graph on the paper comparing the kitchen items you counted.

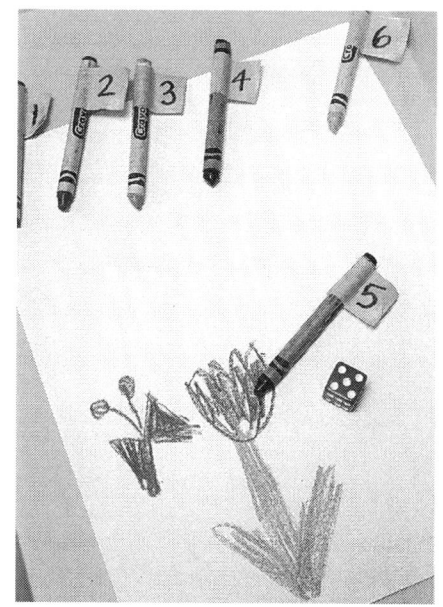

COLOR BY NUMBER

For this activity, you will need six crayons or markers of different colors, some masking o painter's tape, plain paper, and a die. Start by putting a little masking tape on each crayon or marker and labeling it with a number 1-6.
Give your child a piece of paper and a die. Tell them that they can draw anything they want, but they have to stop and roll the die every minute. Whatever number they roll, they must use that color crayon until the next roll.

Make it easier-> Use a coloring sheet and label each section with a number, instead of using a timer, which can be tough for some kids, color until that section is filled. Roll and continue.

Make it harder -> Use two dies, adding them together to get the number. Remember, you will need to increase your crayons or markers from six to twelve.

MATH ACTIVITIES

GO GRAB 10

This is a simple game you can play that gets your child moving as well as learning. It's so simple that you can have older take over if you have something that needs your attention. All you have to do is ask your child, "Go grab 2 books, go grab 3 trucks, go grab 10 socks!"

Make it easier -> Keep the amounts low and the things you have lots of (spoons, shoes, books).

Make it harder -> Ask for larger amounts and make the items harder to find. "Go grab 3 things that are square, go grab 4 soft things, go grab 3 things that start with this sound..."

WHICH HAND HAS MORE?

This is a variation on my husband's game to get my kids to take their vitamins. Pop a few small items like raisins, nuts, fruit snacks... whatever works for your family, into your hands. One hand has to have more than the other. Show both your closed fists to your child and say, "Guess which hand has more!" Open that hand and count. Now open the other hand and count. Which has more? What if you count them all together? What number will you get?

I guess you could do this with small toys, which I would in a classroom, but the food is novel and appropriate for at-home learning. Truth be told, my favorite food to use for this are Skittles. I wouldn't use them every time, but that was definitely a way to make your child want to keep playing.

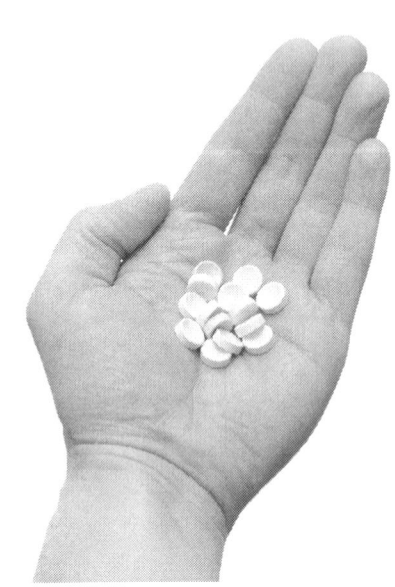

WHO IS THE TALLEST?

Getting taller is an obsession with many kids, because being big aka grown-up is thins somewhat elusive magical idea. If they only knew right ? Use that interest to help them learn some great math skills.

This is all about comparing heights. When your whole family is together (any size of family works!) line up from tallest to shortest. If you have a measuring tape go ahead and measure everyone. Write the measurements down. Look at those numbers together. Which is the biggest? Does the tallest person have the biggest number?

Tuck the paper away and repeat this in a few months. Are the measurements the same? Why, why not?

MATH ACTIVITIES

SHAPE COLLAGE

Math and art come together for this activity that is easily adjusted to fit your child's likes/dislikes and abilities. All you need is some colored paper, scissors, and glue. Cut a bunch of shapes out of colored paper and then glue them on a full sheet of paper. It can be abstract, or your child can use the shapes to make something recognizable. The benefit of this activity is that children can manipulate shapes; we aren't just asking them to memorize shape names; we are offering them a chance to touch, move, and create with them.

Make it easier -> Use 2-3 different shapes.

Make it harder -> Use many different shapes and have your child help you prep the activity with you. They can help draw and cut out the shapes too.

MORE, LESS, OR THE SAME?

When we think about preschool math, we usually focus on recognition activities like naming numbers or shapes, but understanding concepts like more or less is an essential part of math. For this activity, you will want to get two identical containers (glass jars, Tupperware, juice cups) and some water.

Start with two empty containers. Pour a little into one cup, leaving the other empty. Ask them, "Which cup has more?" Discuss their answer briefly. Now fill the second to the same. Ask again. Discuss their answer. Give your child a chance to pour and ask you which has more or less.

Make it easier -> Focus just on more or less.

Make it harder -> Use three cups and use the terms, most and least in addition to more, less and equal.

NICKEL AND DIME SORTING

Sorting is an important activity, and when we focus on size sorting, we help give our children vocabulary and a fundamental understanding of measurement.

You will want three small bowls or containers for this activity and a big handful of coins. Tell your child it's time to separate the coins by size, the larger coins called nickels go in one container, and the smaller dimes in the other. As you sort together, talk about the differences/similarities. They are both round, which is heavier? How do they feel? Are they cold? What if you hold one for a minute, does it warm up? After sorting count, how many nickels and dimes you have in each container.

Make it easier -> Use a limited amount of coins.

Make it harder -> After counting figure out which pile is worth more.

MATH ACTIVITIES

SAME AND DIFFERENT

You will need some paper, scissors, and colorful markers. Fold your paper into four and cut it into four smaller sheets. Cut those sheets in two. You should have eight smaller pieces of paper. Draw 3 to 4 shapes, making one shape different from the others-for example, three red hearts, and one blue circle. Make different combinations of the same and different shapes on the other pieces of paper.

Give your child a marker and ask them to circle the shape that is different from the others. Label it for them if they don't know the shape saying, " Yes, the yellow triangle is different from the three blue circles."

WHICH CAN HOLD MORE?

This builds on the last page's lesson about more and less, but this time it's not about comparing amounts. It is about estimating capacity. It sounds tough, but it's not. Grab 3-4 different size containers (some wide and shallow and some tall and deep) and a large measuring cup filled with water.

Which container holds the most water? Fill and find out. Does the taller one hold more? Explore and have fun!

Make it easier -> Do this at bathtime with plastic containers.

Make it harder -> As you fill each container, take note and write down their exact capacity and place them in order from smallest to largest.

SHAPE SORTING

Grab some construction paper or other craft materials you might have on hand like foam sheets and scissors. Cut out some shapes, I like making them multiple sizes, but you don't have to. Pop them in a big pile and ask your child to help you sort them into individual shape piles. After your sort, count each collection to see which pile has more, less, or if they all have the same number of shapes.

Make it easier -> Use the same color paper for individual shapes, all yellow triangles, all pink squares, all blue hearts, etc. This helps your child use the color as a scaffold (hint).

Make it harder -> After counting, use subtraction to figure out the difference between the estimated and actual amounts.

MATH ACTIVITIES

FRUIT KABOB PATTERNS

Recognizing patterns is foundational for math and reading, but just because it's vital doesn't mean it can't be fun. For this activity, you will need two kinds of fruit, some toothpicks or kabob sticks. Place the fruit (berries, melon chunks, and banana slices work best) in a bowl and tell your child you are going to make kabobs for a snack, but you will try to follow a pattern. A pattern is when items or things repeat in a predictable way, so you can guess what's next. Make a simple ababab pattern with the fruit and ask your child what they think comes next. When I teach patterns, I sing "Blueberry, banana, blueberry, banana..." My students fill in what's next.

Make it easier -> Stick to simple ABAB patterns.

Make it harder -> Try adding in a third fruit and making more complicated patterns.

GRAPHING WITH TOYS

When adults think of graphing, we think of pretty complex graphs, but when children are just learning, we keep things super simple. For this activity, you will need a bunch of toys, but not just any toys. Toys that you can classify, color is a great differentiating factor.
Make a basic graph with painter's tape on carpet or sidewalk chalk outside. Next, add numbers along the y-axis and color names or whatever attribute you are sorting them on the x-axis. Add your toys. Don't forget to count and point out the amount corresponds to the numbers on the y-axis.

Make it easier -> Graph using only two attributes such as red and blue cars.

Make it harder -> Graph using many - red, orange, yellow, green, and blue Lego.

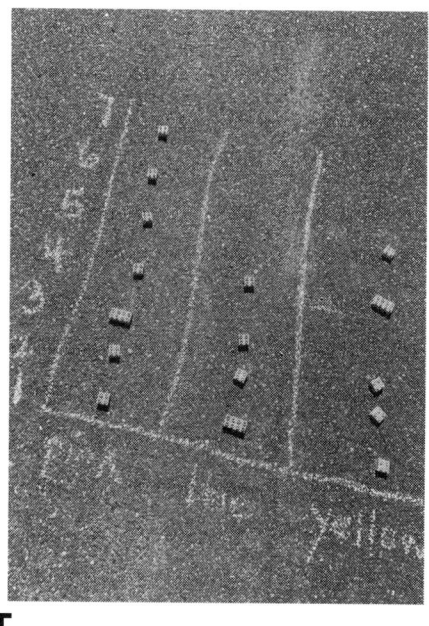

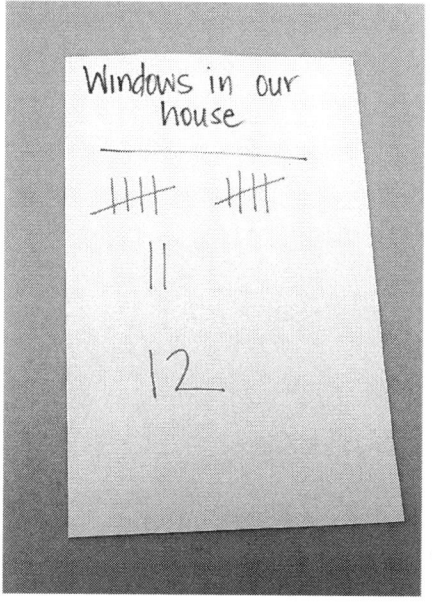

TALLY AND COUNT

Using tally marks is a fun way to represent numbers. It helps us count quickly and efficiently. Learning to recognize amounts without counting, like the dots on dice, fingers on a hand, and tally marks is called subitizing, and this activity helps children with that.

Grab some paper and decide on something to tally. It can be anything from how many birds you see at the window in 10 minutes, cars that drive past your apartment, or how many letters you have in your full name. Use the paper and tally marks to count. Move on to something else.

Make it easier -> Tally and count up to 5 multiple times, so they begin to recognize tally marks for 1-5

Make it harder -> Tally up larger amounts and model counting the tally marks by 5 introducing the idea of skip counting.

MATH ACTIVITIES

MUSICAL NUMBERS

Gather some plain paper and write numbers on them. Use a mix of numbers your child recognizes and some they don't. We want the child to feel confident but also be challenged. Place them around a room with the furniture pushed aside, so there is room to move and groove when the music plays. Play the music and boogie. Pause the music and call out a number. Encourage your child to find and stand on the number you called out. Repeat!

Make it easier -> Use only a few numbers and make them all different colors. When it's time to call out the letter, call it out as" Red 4" or "Blue 2" whatever colors the numbers are. This gives your child help to find the numbers since they can use the color as a hint.

Make it harder -> Use more and larger numbers.

SHAPE HUNT

Make some shapes with paper; squares, circles, ovals, rectangles, stars, hearts, triangles, and crescents. Make at least eight, and hide them around your home.

Now it's time to go hunting. What shapes did you find? As your child finds them ask them this and help label any, they don't know.

Make it easier -> Use only two kinds of shapes, for example, four squares and four triangles.

Make it harder –> Use several different shapes, making some larger and smaller to help your child learn that the shape name is constant even if the size of the shape changes.

ESTIMATION STATION

This doesn't need to be fancy. You just need a few see-through containers or jars and something to fill them. Fill the containers with small items. Ask your child to estimate how many things are in the jars. Write the estimations down; if your child can have them write the numbers down. After everyone estimates, it's time to open them up and count. Write the actual number down too.

I like using lego because after we estimate we can build with the bricks, working on spatial and fine motor skills. Corks, coins, and candies all make great options.

Make it easier -> Use smaller jars/ containers.

Make it harder -> After counting, use subtraction to determine the difference between the estimated and actual amounts.

MATH ACTIVITIES

ROLL & STOMP

Grab some dice and make a space somewhere in your home where your child can move around. This is such a simple math activity, but preschoolers love it.

Now explain that you are going to roll the dice and stomp that many times.

Roll and stomp! Count the dots on the die and then count out each stomp. Mix things up with other movements like jumping, marching with high knees, clapping, and jumping jacks.

Make it easier -> Use a single die.

Make it harder -> use two or more dice and add together before stomping it out.

POST-IT NUMBER LINE

This is a fun and active number recognition and number order activity you can do anywhere. When my kids were little, I'd do this while we were traveling.

Start by writing numbers on your post-its.

Next, hide all but the number one all-around a designated space. Show your child that you have number one, but you need their help to find the next number. Send them off to find it. Pop it in line and keep going until all the numbers are found.

Make it easier -> Use a small group of numbers.

Make it harder –> Go wild and make a number line as long as your child's interest and your pack of post-its will take you!

MEASURE WITH BLOCKS

Non-standard measurement confuses many parents. I like to think of it as a way to compare items. Children don't need to know what a centimeter or an inch is to know that the gourd in this picture is longer than the twig. They can see it, and when they measure with blocks, the gourd uses 15 blocks, and the twig only uses 5.

You can use any items for this activity, and you can use any blocks. Lego, Duplo, Unifix cubes, and wooden blocks are all great. You just have to make sure you are using the same size blocks for all the measuring.

Make it easier -> Keep it simple and measure a few of your child's favorite things.

Make it harder -> Grab some paper and record the measurements. Which is the longest or tallest item on the list? Which is the shortest?

MATH ACTIVITIES

SNACK CRACKER GRAPHING

In my teacher world, this is a classic activity. I sent this activity home during remote learning last year, and I was surprised by how many of my families found it novel.

Get some multi-colored fish crackers. Pop them in a bowl and try not to eat them while making a simple graph with paper and markers. All you need to do is make a column for each color of cracker. Draw a goldfish in the corresponding color at the bottom. Now invite your child to place the crackers in the correct column when your bowl is empty. Count the colors. Which color has the most? Which has the least?

Make it easier -> Graph just a handful of crackers.

Make it harder -> Make predictions before you start placing the crackers on the graph. Count to see if your predictions were right.

NUMBER BOWLING

You don't need a fancy kid bowling set for this activity. You can use empty plastic bottles or even empty paper towel rolls. Using a marker add numbers to the bottles or paper rolls. Try to use lots of numbers your child does know and maybe a few that they are struggling to name. Space the bottles or rolls out because, unlike in real bowling in this game, you don't want your pins to knock other pins down, but if they do, no biggie.

Hand them a ball and yell out a number. It's their job to knock it down.

Make it easier -> Use only 3 bottles/ paper rolls.

Make it harder –> Use many pins and take turns being the caller vs. the bowler.

NUMBER WALK

You can grab this free printable tally sheet(in appendix) or make your own with things to count like cars, people, and stop signs. Use whatever you are likely to see and be able to count wherever you are walking. Keep count on the sheet, and then write the number in the box when you have finished your walk.

Make it easier -> Skip the tally sheet and keep count of one thing (like houses or blue cars) as you walk.

Make it harder -> Tally up larger amounts and model counting the tally marks by 5. This will introduce them to skip counting. They do not need to be able to do this yet. It's just an introduction.

MATH ACTIVITIES

NATURE NUMBER LINE

Grab some sidewalk chalk and write some numbers in a line. I'd start with 1-10. Then invite your child to find objects in nature to complete the line. 1 rock, 2 leaves, 3 sticks... etc...

Make it easier -> keep it simple, 1-5.

Make it harder -> Is your child capable of skip counting (counting by 2s or 5s?) if so make the line using those numbers (2, 4, 6, 8...). to help them continue learning at their pace.

WHO HAS THE BIGGEST?

Who has the biggest boots? What about the biggest bed? Who has the biggest pants? There are so many objects in your home that you can use to help learn this concept and practice this mathematical vocabulary. Make a simple list of these questions, and then go find the objects and determine who in your family has the biggest.

Make it easier -> Use only 3 or 4 items.

Make it harder -> Add in the idea of smallest and medium.

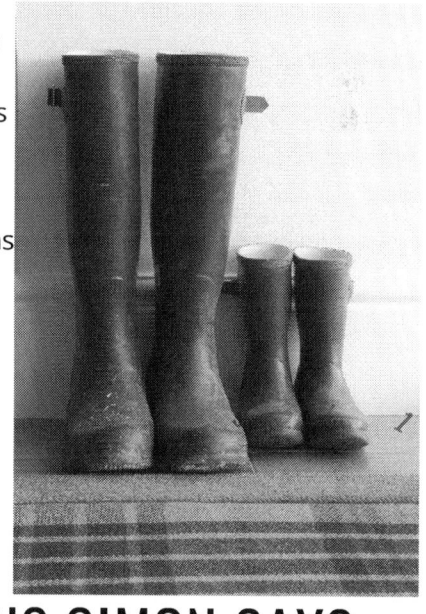

PUDDLE POSITIONS SIMON SAYS

Positional words are important for spatial skill development. Kids can't understand positions if they don't have the common vocabulary to explore them. This game is a fun way to learn, and you don't have to use a puddle. It's way more fun if you do.

After it rains pop outside and tell your kiddo that you are going to play Simon Says with this puddle. Go over positions you can be in with the puddle (next to/ beside, in front, behind, in).

Now it's time to play.

Give them commands like "Simon says stand next to the puddle, stand behind the puddle, jump in front of the puddle, jump IN the puddle!

MATH ACTIVITIES

FLIP & MOVE

I love using movements along with counting because it helps reinforce the idea of one-to-one correspondence. As you count, you touch items, or in this case, you move your body with every number.

Grab some paper, cut into small squares, and write numbers on half of them them. On the other half, write movements. Jump, stomp, hop on one foot, clap, etc...

Shuffle each pile and place them face down. Flip one square from each. Call out the number and the movement.

Make it easier -> Stick to small numbers.

Make it harder -> Write only large numbers and have fun working up a sweat stomping 25 times, jumping 15, and hopping on one foot 30 times! This is a great way to work off extra energy.

SPRAY THE SHAPE

Sidewalk chalk is a wonderful tool for all kinds of learning. For this activity, use it to make shapes on your sidewalk or driveway. Hand your child a spray bottle or squirt gun. Call out the shape and have them spray it.

Make it easier -> Keep it simple with basic shapes like circles, triangles, and squares.

Make it harder -> Add in ovals, octagons, pentagons, and a rhombus!

ROLL A MONSTER

I know I said you wouldn't need any special materials, and this photo is of my at preschool version of this activity - let me share a much simpler one for you. You'll need a piece of paper, colored pencils (one lighter color like hot pink, lime green, etc..) and one dark. Draw a monster with a mouth but NO eyes.

Tell your child you need help drawing the monster's many eyes. Hand them the die and tell them to roll it and then add that many eyes. Keep going! If you have googly eyes handy, grab some and add those instead of drawing them on. Either way, your child will be working on wonderful fine motor skills in addition to math ones.

Make it easier -> Make a small monster and use only one die.

Make it harder -> Use two dice. Roll and add the sum of the two dice together and add that many eyes to your monster.

SCIENCE ACTIVITIES

Don't be intimidated by trying to make science simple enough for preschool, Just think of it as curiosity, observation, and problem-solving. You might not have all these supplies at home, but they can easily be found at a grocery store

SCIENCE ACTIVITIES

ALIVE OR NOT?

Go for a walk and ask your child to help you decide what is living and what isn't. Is a plant alive? What about a car? A rock? A bird? What do things need to do to be alive? They need to be able to grow, use something for fuel, and reproduce. Can a car grow? Can a rock? What about a baby bird or that little tree?

Make it easier –> Keep the lesson short – only talk about one or two characteristics of living things.

Make it harder –> After talking about how plants are alive, try planting a seed and watching it grow together over the next many weeks. What does it need to stay alive? Research how it can reproduce.

WHAT WILL FREEZE FIRST?

Find an ice cube tray that you aren't using and 4-10 different liquids from around your home. Things like water, juice, tomato sauce, chocolate sauce, ketchup, milk, paint whatever you have on hand. Pour a little into the ice cube tray. Together with your child, make predictions about which you think will freeze first. Observe and discuss your findings.

Make it easier -> Use fewer liquids.

Make it harder -> Make a simple chart and record your observations. Observe the tray every 30 minutes.

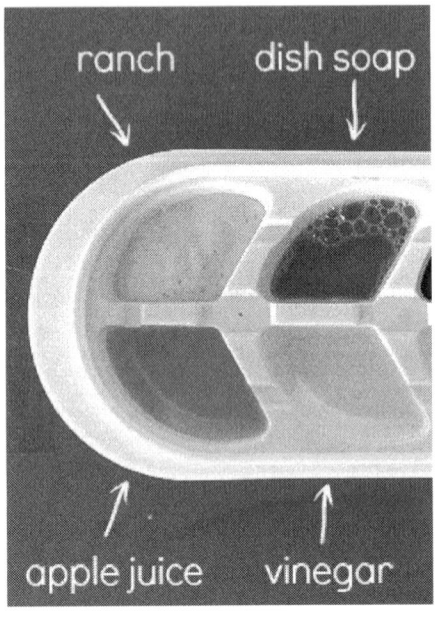

SINK OR FLOAT

Get a tub of water and fill it up. A large mixing bowl will work fine, so will a bathtub! Gather various toys or household items you don't mind getting wet. Try to get a mix of things; some that will float and some that won't.

Hold up the items one at a time, asking your child if they think it will stay on the water and float or fall to the bottom and sink. Place each item in one at a time. Was your child's prediction, right?

Make it easier –> use items that they have seen floating or sinking like rocks and bath toys. This will encourage them to speak up and make a prediction because many of theirs will be right!

Make it harder –> Ask your child why they think some float and some sink.

SCIENCE ACTIVITIES

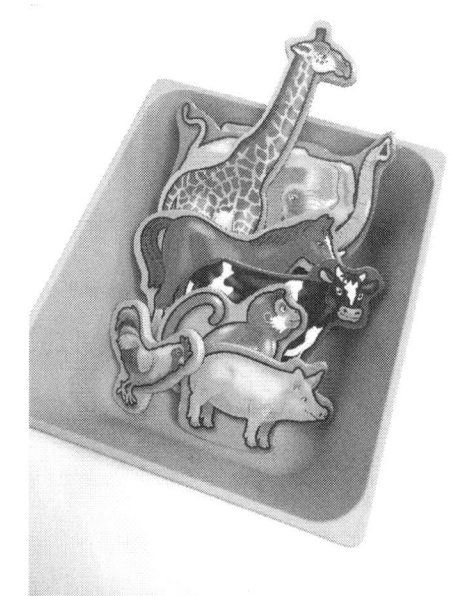

ANIMAL SOUNDS

Go through your toy box or child's room to find some animal toys pop them in a bag or other place your child can't see them.

Ask your child to close their eyes and use their sense of hearing for this game. Make the sound the animal toy you have in your hand makes. For example, for a toy cow, you would moo.

Have your child yell out what animal makes that sound and then open their eyes to see if they are correct.

WHAT'S THE WEATHER?

Checking the weather can be a daily activity that you work into your routine or like everything else used when the time is right. I like to do this activity outside, so children can see and feel the weather. Ask your child to be your meteorologist and tell you what the weather is like right now, then ask them for a prediction for how the weather might or might not change.

Make it easier –> Sing the weather song. The song guides the children and makes the activity quick and fun! The lyrics are in the appendix.

Make it harder –> After making your forecast come inside, fold a piece of paper in half and draw the weather now on one side and the prediction for later on the other.

BEAN SPROUTING

This is more of a long term project, but making it and checking in on it every few days is a great way to work science into any routine. All you need is a dried bean, some dirt, and a plastic bottle. Cut the plastic bottle in two and fill with soil. Add the bean, so it is against the side of the bottle, so you can observe it's growth. Water it. Place it by a window where it can get sunlight. Re-dampen the dirt when it gets dry. Observe as it sprouts.

Make it easier -> this is pretty straight forward.

Make it harder -> Create a simple observation log and have your child draw a picture of the sprout every few days to track the changes.

SCIENCE ACTIVITIES

COLOR MIXING

Color mixing is so much fun with preschoolers who are still wowed by this sort of experiment. Gather up some glass jars, food color, and water. Set aside one jar as the mixing jar. Add a few drops of different food color in each jar, and fill with water. Now it's time to pour a little from different jars into the mixing jar to see what color it will create.

Make it easier -> Take this outside or to the bath where a little mess is less stressful for everyone.

Make it harder -> Make predictions before you mix the colors, and if you want to record the color "recipes" with crayons or markers in a simple chart.

WHAT WILL MOLD FIRST?

This is another longer-term science activity that preschoolers think is pretty rad. You might think it's pretty gross, but a lot of parenting is, and this is educational, so just do it. You will need 3-5 zip locks and food. I used plastic test tubes, but bags work just as well. It can be any food. Bread, fruit, cheese, and cold cuts are easy to put in a bag. All you have to do it pop them in the bags and leave them to mold.

Over the next week, watch how they change, which molded first? Do they stink? Whatever you do, don't open the bags, just trust me on that one, especially if you use milk.

Make it easier -> Use two types of food and compare how they mold.

Make it harder -> Use many types of food and keep a simple observation log with written descriptions of your observations.

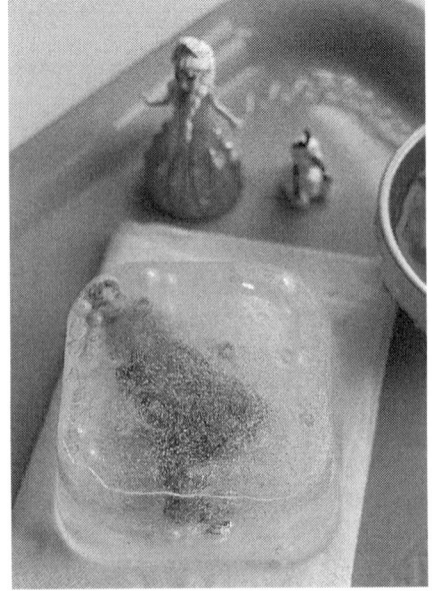

MELT THE ICEBERG

This is a great activity to do outside on a warm day. You get your little one a little vitamin D, but you also get to step away from work or other responsibilities and get outside. Of course, it can be done inside too.

The night before you plan on doing this activity with your child, find a plastic tub, fill it with water, pop in a few toys like Duplo or action figures, and freeze it.

When it's time to play, get a few mugs of warm water, spoons, turkey baster, or pipettes if you happen to have them. Use the warm water and tools to free the toys from the iceberg!

Make it easier -> Freeze smaller items in an ice cube tray.

SCIENCE ACTIVITIES

MAGIC FLOWERS

These aren't real magic flowers; they are color-changing, though.

This science activity is a fun way to show children the functions of stems and the capillary action inside. All you need are some white flowers (carnations work well), glass vases or jars, food color, and water.

Pop the flowers in the jars and make predictions about what will happen. Check-in with the flowers, and when they start changing colors, ask your child how they think this happened. Explain how the stem acts like a straw that sucks up the water and moves it around to all the parts of the flower that need it.

SWIM, FLY, OR WALK

Part of science is learning to observe and use those observations to make sense of things. In this case, children look at images or figurines of animals and think, do they swim, fly, or walk to get around?

Gather up animal toys from around your house, three pieces of paper, and marker. Write swim, fly, walk on one paper, and spread them on a table or the floor. Now it's time to examine each animal toy and decide if they fly, swim, or walk?

When you are done, count each group. If you don't have enough toys for this activity, there is a link in the appendix to a free printable with photos of animals.

MAGNET EXPLORATION

At preschool, we have many rad and costly magnetic exploration tools for our science center. But you don't need anything fancy to learn.

You do need a magnet, and yes, fridge magnets will work just fine. You will also need a piece of paper and a marker. Use the paper to make a simple chart. Pop a checkmark and an x at the top, and a line down the middle. You are ready to explore.

Walk around your home and explore what the magnet will stick to and what it won't. Draw a simple picture or write down the names of the items in the appropriate column when you are done, look at what the items in each column have in common.

SCIENCE ACTIVITIES

FOLLOW THE SHADOW

This activity brings gross motor and science together. You will need to do this on a sunny day to create shadows on the patio walk or other surfaces. Start wiggling your arms and ask your child if they know what is making this shadow. Explain that your bodies are blocking the sunlight from shining on the surface. When the light can't touch the surface, you get a shadow.

Now it's time to play!

Move around and ask your child to follow the movements that your shadow is making, so their shadow follows. Take turns being the leader!

NATURE TOWERS

Children love to build and knock down towers, and there is no reason you can do this outside. If you have access to a yard or park, spend some time gathering items that might make functional natural blocks like big sticks, rocks, large pieces of mulch, etc.

Next, it's time to build. Building towers like this is a lot more complicated than most people realize and requires problem-solving and trial and error. It's basic engineering!

If you don't have access to a yard or park, you can buy rocks online, and after you use them for this engineering activity, get some paint pens and decorate for an easy art project!

BUG HUNT

This is not a bug hunt and KEEP activity. No bugs will be permanently adopted into your home unless you want that. This is more like a bug safari where you go searching for bugs but leave them right where you found them. If you have a magnifying glass or even binoculars, those can help set the stage for a fun, active science activity.

Grab some paper and with your child brainstorm all the bugs you think you might find in your yard or at the park. Next, head outside and start hunting out a tally mark next to each bug that you see.

After the hunt, count up the tally marks and talk about which bugs were your child's favorite or least favorite. Have your child draw a picture of their favorite bug.

SCIENCE ACTIVITIES

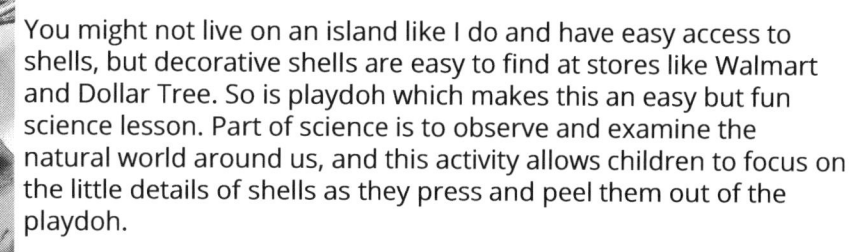

SHELL PLAYDOUGH FOSSILS

You might not live on an island like I do and have easy access to shells, but decorative shells are easy to find at stores like Walmart and Dollar Tree. So is playdoh which makes this an easy but fun science lesson. Part of science is to observe and examine the natural world around us, and this activity allows children to focus on the little details of shells as they press and peel them out of the playdoh.

If you have the time or inclination, you can dive deeper into what a fossil is and how they are formed in nature. If not, that's fine. Your child will still be developing important skills with the basic activity.

NATURE TABLE

If you have decided to homeschool your child for a significant length of time I encourage you to create a nature table with changing "exhibits" throughout the year. You don't need to spend any money on this other than investing in a magnifying glass (psst! Dollar Tree has them) and some time finding bits of nature to bring inside to explore. Here is a list of some things I have had on my nature table over the years:

apples	pinecones
leaves	birds nests (abandoned)
pumpkins	sea glass
shells	crab shells
rocks	flowers
seeds	plant starts

WHICH ONE IS VINEGAR?

You don't have to commit to making baking soda and vinegar volcanos to explore simple eruptions. If the idea of this mess freaks you out, take a breath and follow these steps.

Grab four small containers, I use small mason jars, but anything will work. Add baking soda to 2. Now add water and white vinegar to the other. Explain to your child that when some things mix, there are reactions. You will see what happens when water and baking soda mix, and then vinegar and baking soda mix.

Why did the vinegar and baking soda make so many bubbles but the water didn't? Keep your explanation simple. Water and vinegar are made up of different chemicals. The chemicals in vinegar and the chemicals in the baking soda react to each other bubbling up, but the ones in the water and baking soda don't.

SCIENCE ACTIVITIES

SHAVING CREAM & POOL NOODLE TOWERS

I created this activity when I couldn't find the little foam blocks I usually use with shaving cream, and my students loved it. This might technically be an engineering project, but I think of engineering as in the sciences, so I'm popping it here.

Get a pool noodle and slice it into pieces. I used a serrated kitchen knife. Now it's time to add some shaving cream and build. Encourage your child to test out different positions for the noodles. Can they stay on their side? What happens if they use more shaving cream or less? Get them in the testing mindset as they build and watch them blossom as little engineers.

PLUG YOUR NOSE AND TASTE

Yes, this is a taste test with a twist. How much of taste is dependent on smell? Let's find out! This is a great snack time activity.

Gather up a few distinctly flavored foods with the same texture - yogurt, ice cream, pouched fruit sauce, even fruit leather. Show them to your child. Explain to them that they need to guess the flavor only using their sense of taste.

Close their eyes, plug their nose, and taste!

Now keep their eyes closed and unplug their nose, and taste again.

Was it easier the 2nd time?

Keep going with the other flavors.

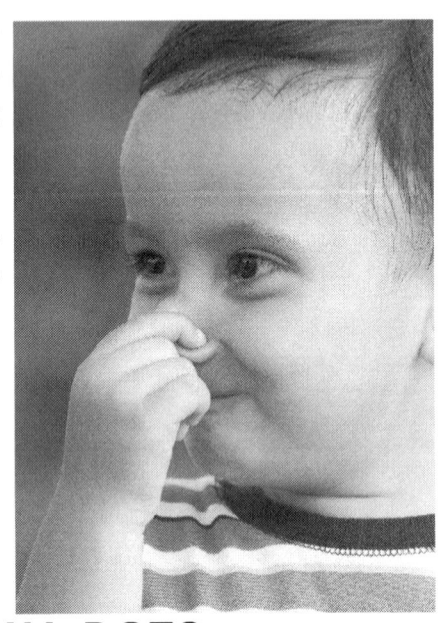

OIL & WATER POLKA DOTS

Water and oil don't mix. As adults, we know that. Young children don't. This activity, lovingly called "polka dots" by my then 3-year-old daughter, helps to introduce the idea that oil and water don't mix.

All you need is some oil, water, and food color. We used a little eyedropper, but your smallest spoon will work as well. Drop the colored water into the oil and watch what happens.

Here is my *very* basic explanation: Tiny bits of water are attracted to each other, so it sticks together even when immersed in oil. Water is also heavier than oil, so the little polka dots fall to the bottom.

SENSORY PLAY

Sensory play does not automatically mean mess. We have five senses, and all five need time to be explored, and you don't need fancy equipment to do it.

SENSORY PLAY

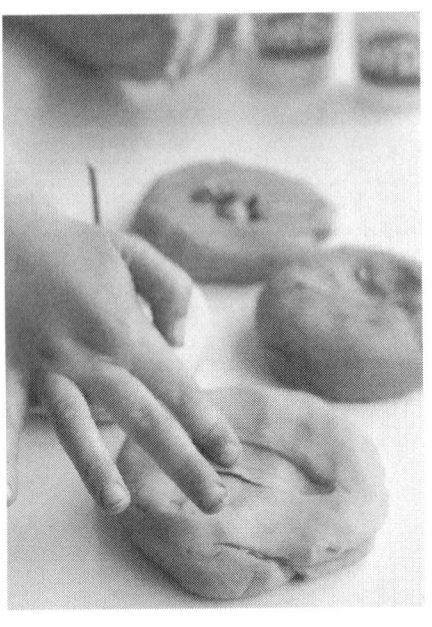

PLAYDOUGH PRINTS

This activity is more than just a sensory activity, as children are observing nature and working on fine motor skills too. It is always fun because it changes based on what sort of leaves you have. All you need is some playdough and leaves or other bits of nature. Press it in and peel it back, voila you have a very cool leaf print in your playdough. It's best if you do this when leaves aren't too dry or brittle.

Make it easier -> This one is pretty simple but use larger leaves with younger students.

Make it harder-> Go for a walk together and try to find a leaf that will make the most interesting print.

THAT'S SMELLY!

Go around your home and find 5-10 items with strong smells.

Cosmetics, food, spices, flowers from your garden, unlit candles, kid-safe scented markers, and stinky shoes are good examples. Anything safe to smell is fair game. Stay away from cleaners or anything that has fumes like glue or magic markers. We want this activity to build brain cells, not kill them.

After you have gathered the items together, smell each one, and decide if it's a good or bad smell. Choose your favorite and least favorite scent.

KITCHEN SINK WATER TABLE

Water is magical. It is so calming for wound up preschoolers. I don't expect you all to have a water table at home, but if you do skip the kitchen sink and bust that bad boy out.

If you don't have one, your sink will do the trick, but first, disinfect it. Kitchen sinks are germ factories, so clean the sink and dry it thoroughly before filling it back up for play.

After you do fill it up, add in some tools like measuring cups, corks, big serving spoons, soup ladles, and plastic bowls. Invite your child to come to explore.

SENSORY PLAY

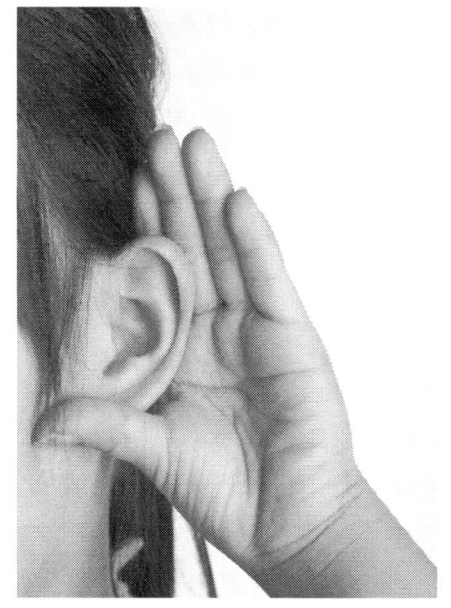

SOUND SAFARI

Go outside with your child. Close your eyes and ask your child to tell you what they hear. If you can go for a walk, go around your neighborhood. Keep a mental note of all the sounds heard in your neighborhood. Come back inside and draw those sounds and what was making them; birds, trucks, construction, maybe a siren, or a dog barking.

Make it easier –> you can't just roll with this and take some time to listen and breathe calmly.

Make it harder –> Talk about what your child heard. Talk about which sound was the quietest and which was the loudest.

COOKIE CUTTER PLAYDOUGH PLAY

Cookie cutters are a great tool to have if you are learning at home. This activity is all about pushing and squeezing and digging and pressing into the playdough. The cookie cutters help us do that.

When children play with playdough, they work on building hand strength, explore their senses, and get some of their sensory needs met. The squeezing, pressing, and squishing helps children get the sensory input they need, and that is why playdough is often so calming to young kids. The cookie cutters help us get started and settled in this activity.

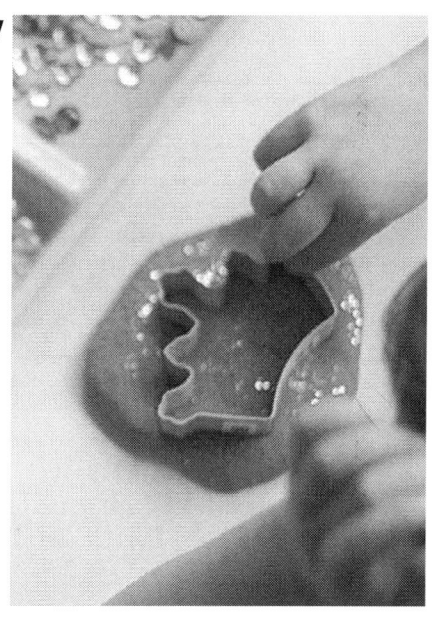

BUBBLE BIN

This activity is smelly, novel to look at, makes fun sounds, and has multiple textures to feel. Whisking up the bubbles is also great for developing coordination and the arm and shoulder muscles that our kids need for all sorts of vital tasks.

All you need is a bin, water, some dish soap (make sure it's not one that will irritate your child's skin), and a whisk. Add a little dish soap to the water and hand your child the whisk.

Food color is a fun add-in but not required.

SENSORY PLAY

TEXTURE HUNT

This can be done inside on a rainy day or outside when the weather is nice. It requires NO supplies other than things to touch. Tell your child you will hunt for things today, but you are not just using your eyes to find them. You will also use your fingers. You are looking for things that feel different.

Can you find something soft? What about prickly? Can you find something smooth? Can you find something rough? What about squishy?

POTATO SCRUB A DUB DUB

Scrubbing dirt off of potatoes seems like a menial task for some, but it's a fun preschool activity that helps build hand strength and meets sensory needs as well. Children love to see the potato get clean as they rub the shin with a kitchen scrubber.

The best part is that after they are clean, you get to cook!

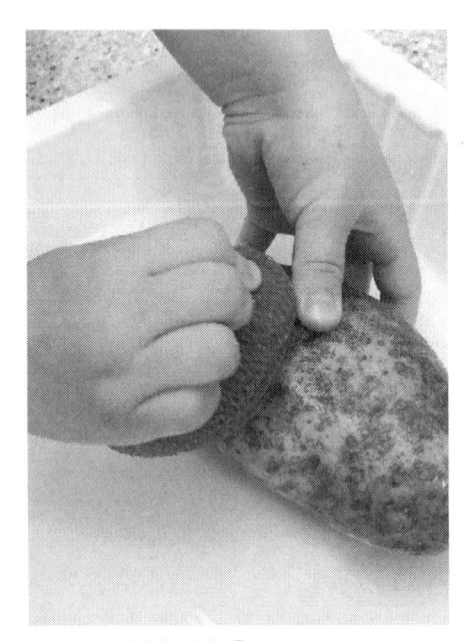

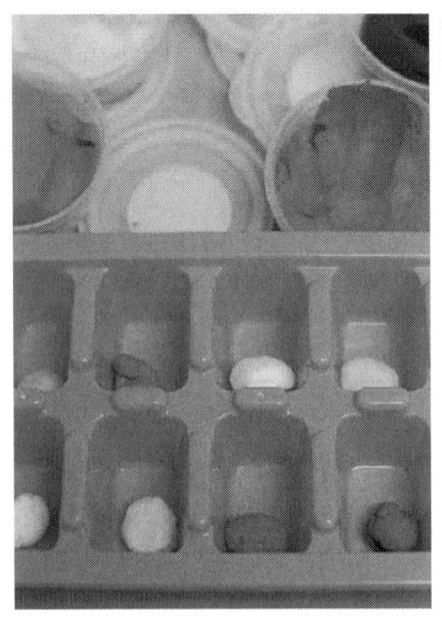

PLAYDOUGH COLOR MIXING

Let them mix the colors!

At least pinch off a little play dough, place it in an ice cube tray and let them squish the playdough together to create a whole new color. As they are learning how colors mix to make new colors, they are also working on important fine motor skills and getting a great sensory experience while doing so.

SENSORY PLAY

GUESS THE SOUND

Go through your toy box or child's room to find some toys that make distinctive sounds (stuffed dogs, toy ambulances, hammers). Then pop them in a bag or other place your child can't see them.

Ask your child to join you and to close their eyes. Explain that they will be using only their sense of hearing for this game. Now it's time for you to make the sound the toy you have in your hand makes. For example, for a toy cow, you would moo, make a siren sound for a police car, etc... Have your child yell out what makes that sound and then open their eyes to see if they are correct. Repeat.

FRUIT TASTE TEST

Use what you have. You don't need exotic fruit for this activity. Apples and bananas work great! You do need at least two kinds of fruit, some paper, and a pencil or marker.

Start by making a simple chart with the paper with the name of the fruit and space for your child to draw a happy or sad face after they taste it.

Next up, taste the fruit on the list and decide whether it gets a happy or sad face?

SUPER SIMPLE SENSORY BIN

Sensory play is a staple in any preschool classroom, and you can recreate this at home using everyday materials. Grab a plastic bin, like a sizeable glad ware container, and fill it with dry rice, popcorn kernels, or beans. Add some fun spoons, cups, and scoops, and you are good to go if you want to add in things to hide and find, like bug figurines, blocks, and other little toys.

Explore filling the cups, pouring, and playing. When play is done, store it in a large Ziploc.

*Do not use dry kidney beans. They can be toxic.

SENSORY PLAY

MAKE A MEAL TOGETHER

We forget how vital learning simple tasks like making lunch is. Children love learning practical things, and making a meal together teaches real-life skills while focusing on connection. Chop some fruit, make a simple sandwich, or maybe some pasta together.

Make it easier -> Choose a familiar or favorite food like a PB & J and focus on just spending time together.

Make it harder -> Try a NEW recipe, or bake some cookies after a basic lunch.

PAINTING WITH SOUND

I know I promised that these activities use everyday materials - this is an exception to that rule. For this activity, you will need some jingle bells (they are in any craft store or section of a big box store), paper, paint, paintbrushes, and some ribbon or chenille stems. Thread the jingle bells onto the chenille stem or ribbon and tie them on to the end of your paintbrushes.

Now it's time to paint. As children paint, the jingle bells will jingle and make fun sounds. Ask your child what happens if they paint slower or faster?

STICKER I-SPY

Gather up some stickers and a piece of paper. Have your child help you add the stickers to the paper. After they are all added, play I-spy with the stickers. " Can you find the star sticker?" "Can you find a sticker that rhymes with bar?" Adjust your questions to your child's ability.

Make it easier -> Space out the stickers and only use about 10.

Make it harder -> use a large piece of paper and cover it with stickers spaced closely together.

ART ACTIVITIES

You don't need to spend a bunch of money on expensive art supplies or spend all day creating Pinterest-worthy craft projects to meet your child's needs. For a list of simple supplies, you should have on hand, flip to the appendix.

ART ACTIVITIES

SPONGE PAINTING

School supply stores sell expensive sponges shaped like everything you can think of, but there is no need to be fancy. Grab a few new kitchen sponges and cut them into basic shapes like rectangles, triangles, and squares. Put a thin layer of paint on a plate, give your child a blank sheet of paper, and you have a fantastic art activity that also works on shape recognition.

Make it easier -> This is very basic, but larger shapes are easier for younger children to manipulate.

Make it harder -> Ask your child if they can use the shapes to make something recognizable or make a pattern?

COOKIE CUTTER PRINTING

Most of us have a few cookie cutters lying around, and they are an excellent tool for art! Gather up some fun cookie cutters, some paint, a plate for the paint, and paper. Spread the paint thinly on the plate and place the cookie cutters in it. Print on the paper. Voila, a super fun shape!

Make it easier -> Don't direct anything other than how to make the prints on the paper. Let your child explore the paint and shapes freely.

Make it more complex -> Turn your prints into characters with the addition of googly eyes or even just markers to add a face, arms, and legs.

SIDEWALK CHALK SELF PORTRAITS

On a sunny day, pop outside for this activity. All you need are some sidewalk chalks. Have your child lay down and trace their body on the pavement with sidewalk chalk. Have the dress themselves and make features.

Make it easier ->Instead of a whole body, just do faces!

Make it more complex -> Instead of coloring in clothes draw in bones or organs! Add a heart, a brain, lungs, and more.

ART ACTIVITIES

FREE ART STATION

Free art is precisely what it sounds like a time to explore with whatever materials you have on hand with no adult plan at all. Setting this up as a station in our home for your child to use at their leisure is excellent art option.

Gather your art supplies and create a little station with paper, crayons, stickers, glue, paint, kid scissors, stamps, and recyclables to create with.

Having a placemat is a great way to establish a boundary for where you want your child to create and where messes should stay. When my children were small, I'd tape ours down with painter's tape to keep it from slipping on the table.

EDIBLE SELF PORTRAITS

On a busy day, use lunchtime for art time. This activity can be done in many ways. My favorite is to grab a tortilla or some crackers, cream cheese, some veggies like cucumber, red pepper, raisins, cheese cut into shapes, etc.

Give your child the tortilla spread with the cream cheese (peanut butter and other spreads work well too) and the toppings on the side. Tell your child you are making faces with food, and they can make themselves or create a creature from their imagination with the food.

Make it easier ->Make it together!

Make it harder: Have your child help you prep the activity by chopping veggies, spreading the cream cheese, etc.

NATURE RUBBINGS

You probably did this as a child, and your child may have done this before too. It's a classic art activity that makes getting some fresh air part of the fun.

Pop outside and gather some leaves of different shapes. Now grab some plain white printer paper, and a crayon or two. Have your child help you peel the paper off the crayon (this is wonderful for their fine motor development), place a leaf under the paper (vein side up), and rub the crayon sideways over the leaf. Repeat with the other leaves and different color crayons.

Make it harder -> After making the rubbings find some scissors and cut the rubbings out.

ART ACTIVITIES

MAKE YOUR OWN PUFFY PAINT

This puffy paint is a wonderfully sensory art experience that children love creating from start to finish as long as your child doesn't mash the paint excessively (and some do, and that's fine). It will dry puffy.

Recipe:

3 parts shaving cream - use old-school white shaving cream.
1 part white glue.

You can add a dash of paint for color too!

PLAYDOUGH COLOR MATCHING

The only supplies this activity requires are lots of playdough colors and what I like to call bits and bobs. Buttons, cut pieces of plastic straws, beads... basically anything small.

I could have put this activity in the sensory or fine motor section of this book, but the emphasis on color lead me to pop it here! The main thing your child is doing is color matching, but this is a novel way to do it that really encourages your child to decide which color the bits and bobs belong squished into, and they use lots of fine motor skills while doing it.

PAPER PLATE RAINBOW

Use leftover paper plates from your summer picnics for this simple art activity.

The rainbow pictured was painted with a .99 cent watercolor set, but you can use whatever materials you have on hand. Crayons are wonderful, markers work, and for the brave ones out there, glue and glitter!

If you want to work on your child's hand strength, give them strips of paper and have them tear pieces off, and glue them onto the plate to make a collaged rainbow.

ART ACTIVITIES

SALAD SPINNER ART

I'm not sure I have ever used my salad spinner for salad. I have definitely used it for painting.

Cut some plain paper to fit inside your salad spinner. Pop a sheet in and add some liquid paint.

Cover and spin! Have fun with different color combinations too.

When you have spun all your part for the day, rinse with warm water leaving little in your spinner, ad a drop of dish soap, cover, and spin up some bubbles for extra fun!

NATURE PRINTS

Using novel items in the place of paintbrushes helps children learn to think outside the box. Essentially it promotes creativity. Let them decide what flowers they want to use in place of a paintbrush, and then create! You can give your child flowers to paint with, but I prefer to hand them scissors and go into our garden.

If the flower didn't work so well, go outside and see what other things right be better suited... maybe a twig or large leaf would be better!

PAINT OUTSIDE LIKE MONET

Take art outside and offer your child a chance to paint like the impressionists did, en plein air.

Which is just French for "open-air."

Yes, this is simple, but I hope that it gives your child a chance to look at the things outside in a new way, express themselves through art, and on some of the skills they will need to tackle handwriting when it's time.

ART ACTIVITIES

TRUCK TRACK PAINTING

Dig through the toy box and find the toys with the coolest wheels and tracks for this activity. Also, make sure they are easily washable.

Grab a few plates, some paper (I use the flip side of extra wrapping paper), and of course, paint. Smear some paint on the plates and plop the trucks in. Roll them on the paper and watch as they leave paint tracks behind.

SHELL PAINTING

We've already established that you don't have to live near the ocean to have access to shells, just by a Walmart. Of course, if you do live near an ocean, please do get some fresh air and find some shells. Wash and dry them before painting.

I use watercolors but you can use any paint you have. My kids always liked to paint, wash and repeat. Some of the watercolors' color is retained but most washes off.

SHAPE HOUSE CRAFT

I haven't included many crafts in this book because children need many more opportunities for process art than they do for crafts. That said, crafts serve a purpose, and when they are coupled with things like the opportunity to manipulate shapes and create something meaningful, it's a win.

This shape house craft encourages children to create their homes using shapes. Use whatever art supplies you have on hand, but you will definitely need some sturdy paper, glue, and scissors. For little ones who haven't mastered scissors yet, have pre-cut shapes for them to build their house with. This is a great way to use up scrap paper.

When they are done, ask them about who lives in the house and to tell you a story all about them.

ART ACTIVITIES

PEG DOLL FAMILIES

I wasn't going to include this art activity in this book because peg dolls (old-fashioned clothespins) weren't easily accessible, but now every dollar store I have been to in a year has them. So I am calling that an easy to find everyday material. You will need some of those and some Sharpies.

Wait. Sharpies? Yes. Young children usually rise to the occasion and use materials meant for adults with care. I still recommend *very* close supervision.

Encourage your child to create a whole family and then play with them, creating stories as they do.

PAPER BAG JELLY FISH

Set aside a few lunch-size paper bags next time you are packing lunches for this fun art project. I love any craft that doubles as a toy to play with and develop skills, like storytelling, which these jellyfish certainly do.

First, you will want to paint the paper bags and let them dry.
Next, cut long strips from the bag's opening to about 2/3rds of the way up. Now add a face and play!

For extra fun, add some glitter in the paint and mix before painting. I promise glitter is fun, as long as you don't mind it sticking around forever. If you have googly eyes, go ahead and use them, but a black marker will work well as long as the paint is dry.

WINDOW EASELS

Using a window as an easel not only offers your child a chance at working on a vertical surface, it's also visually appealing. Get some painter's tape and paper and make your window easel now!

You will be amazed at how much longer your child stays engaged when the light streams through their painting.

ART ACTIVITIES

PARALLEL DRAWINGS

This simple activity is a favorite in my preschool class, and it's perfect for a quick art activity on a busy day. To prep, all you need to do is grab some crayons and painter's tape. Tape pairs of crayons together. Offer these novel art tools to your child with some paper and explore.

Make it easier ->This one is so simple there is no need.

Make it harder -> Explore making different shapes and how the taped together crayons make two lines that always stay apart.

KITCHEN TOOL PRINTS

Your kitchen is packed with art tools. Potato mashers make incredible prints, so do glass sponges and dish scrubbers. Choose a tool or two, get some paper, paint, and a plate. Spread the paint on the plate, dip the tools in the paint, and print on the paper.

Make it easier -> Like most art projects, there is no need to simplify.

Make it harder -> Start with two colors of paint and mix to create a new color before printing.

MAGIC PAINTING

Did you know that when watercolors and crayons come together, they make magic? All you need is a white crayon, white paper, a paintbrush, and dark watercolors.

Start by making a drawing on the paper with the white crayon, press hard. Next, it's time to paint watercolors all over the paper to reveal the white crayon underneath.

Make it easier -> Use small pieces of paper to make it easier to cover the space with crayon markings and paint.

Make it harder -> With older children, try writing letters or sight words to read as they are revealed. There is a list of sight words in the appendix.

ART ACTIVITIES

FAMILY PORTRAIT

Family portraits are always a meaningful art activity for children. All you need is paper and a pencil. Take a few moments to talk about your family, how every family is unique, family names, and the difference between immediate and extended families.

Make it easier -> Draw with your child and show your child that this doesn't have to be perfect!

Make it harder -> If you have more time, make a simple frame by painting some cardboard and then gluing the paper on top.

SQUISH PAINTING

This is so much fun and can easily be kept simple, or you can add extras like googly eyes to turn the squish painting into monsters, bugs, or animals.

Start by folding a sheet of plain paper in two. Paint one side. Fold and rub. Open and reveal. Talk about how the painting is perfectly symmetrical, which means the same on both sides.

Make it easier -> Use a small amount of paint, so the squishing doesn't get too messy.

Make it harder -> After your painting dries grab some glue and add googly eyes, use markers to add arms, legs, or antenna!

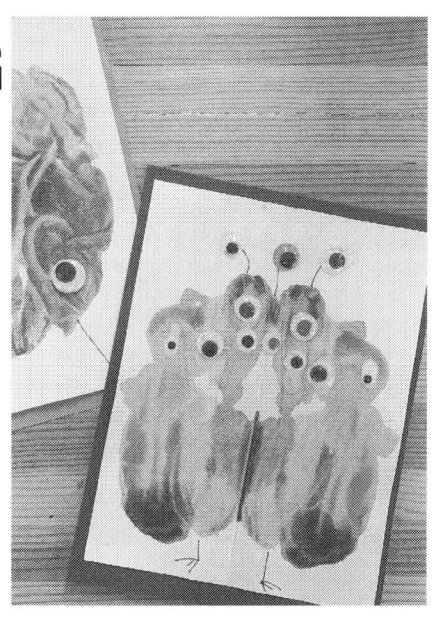

TAPE COLLAGES

Washi tape, duct tape, and colored masking tape are all pretty easy to find online or at office supply stores. This activity uses fun tape-all tape is fun for kids- and lets children create with it. While they do, they are tapping into their creativity, but they are also working on vital fine motor skills as they rip, cut, and place the tape on the paper. All you need is some tape and paper.

Make it easier -> Pre-cut the tape and place pieces on the edge of a table or tray for children not yet capable of cutting off pieces themselves.

Make it harder -> Can you make shapes with the tape, a house, a car, a rainbow, whatever your child likes.

ART ACTIVITIES

COLOR COLLAGES

I do color collages often in my classroom as I explore colors with my students. All you need are multiple items of the same color. Things like paper, pom poms, buttons, feathers, pouch lids (those plastic ones), bread bag clips, ribbon, etc. can be glued on paper. Use what you have. After you have gathered the items, give your child some glue and sturdy paper. Let them explore and choose the items they want to glue on their paper. I like this because children see that each color can look and feel a little different, but they are still the same color.

Make it easier -> Brush the glue on the paper with a wide paintbrush or pastry brush and have your child add the items.

Make it harder -> Gather many colors of items and have your child dig through and find the one color you have decided to use to make the collage

DRAW TO MUSIC

This is a fascinating activity because some children get very into it, and for some, it just doesn't click- that's OK. This is a beautiful way of using classical music and art together. All you need are some markers, paper, and something you can play classical music on. I love using Vivaldi's Concerto number 4 for this activity.

Give your child the markers and paper and tell them that you will play some music, and you want them to draw whatever the music makes them feel. Do this activity with them to model, but there is no wrong way to do this, so if you are drawing calmly and your child is furiously making scribbles, that's OK.

Extend this activity-> After drawing, take this activity to the floor. Ask your child to move to the music and dance with them moving your body along with the music as it changes.

VEGGIE PAINTING

Instead of a paintbrush, use parts of veggies to paint! This sensory experience is fun and helps children to think outside the box too.

You don't have to waste food to do this activity - the ends of a celery stalk, an avocado pit, and the stem and leaves of a carrot work just as well as a potato, corn on the cob, or broccoli. Use what you have to spare and what you are comfortable with using for art. Know that exploring food is beneficial to children even if they aren't eating it. Allowing children to touch, smell, and manipulate vegetables helps introduce and spark curiosity about food.

ART ACTIVITIES

CORK PAINTING

I love using corks for art because I always seem to have some on hand, and they make fun circle prints that help to reinforce shape recognition too.

All you need is some paint, a plate, corks, and paper. Dip the corks in the paint, and have fun. They make an excellent sound when you print them on paper adding another layer of sensory exploration.

PAINTING WITH WATER

Did you know you can paint with water on the sidewalk, unpainted wood porches, and fences? It's a fun art activity that is a litter wet, but it won't stain your home or your kid.

Gather some painting tools like bigger brushes, paint rollers, and sponges, and some water. Get painting! It's an excellent activity for a hot sunny day.

POP CAN PAINTING

Got some aluminum cans in your recycling? Then you can do this activity. Grab some paper, paint, a plate, and some duct or painter's tape too. The tape is to cover the hole in the can that has sharp edges. Dip the bottom of the can in the paint and print it on the paper! Next, spread the paint on the plate.

Extend this activity -> After the paint dries, add eyes, and make faces with the circles!

FINE MOTOR ACTIVITIES

Fine motor development is key for being prepared to learn handwriting, but these skills are about so much more than that. They are crucial for self-help skills like buttoning pants, using eating utensils, and more.

FINE MOTOR ACTIVITIES

PLAYDOUGH TREASURE HUNT

Hide small items like buttons, beads, and coins in the playdough and use those fine motor skills to dig them out. You can use an ice cube tray or silicone mold if desired. If you need an excellent playdough recipe, my favorite is in the appendix.

Make it easier -> use more substantial items like small toys, Lego blocks, etc.

Make it harder -> sort the items after digging them out—sort by color or size.

STICKER WALL

Put some paper on your wall. I like to use the backside of cheap wrapping paper. Tape it to the wall using painter's tape. You can alternatively put a sheet of paper on your fridge door and secure it with magnets. Now it's time to add stickers. Any stickers will do, even office supplies like reinforcements, if you are short on stickers.

Make it easier -> Use a smaller piece of paper that won't feel as daunting to fill.

Make it harder -> If you have letter stickers available, have your child try to spell their name.

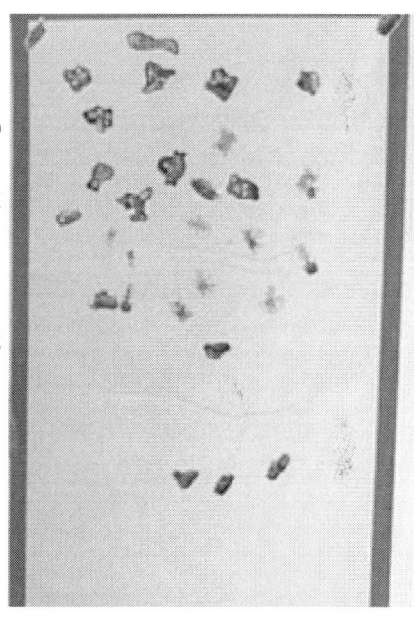

Q-TIP PAINTING

This could be an art project, but it's also fantastic for fine motor development, so I made an executive decision to pop it here. Grab any paint, some paper, and a handful of q-tips. Use the q-tips in place of paintbrushes. Show your child how you can make dots of paint or lines. Encourage your child to hold the q-tips by pinching the stick between their thumb and index finger.

Make it easier -> keep it simple, and use a small piece of paper, so your child doesn't feel like they need to fill a huge piece of paper with paint.

Make it harder-> write out a letter, number, or child's name and trace it with dots of paint.

FINE MOTOR ACTIVITIES

BEAD COLOR SORTING

Gather some pony beads (if you don't have any, you can use colored paper and cut it into tiny pieces), a bowl, and a muffin tin or small jars. Place all the beads (or small squares of paper) mixed in the dish. Now it's time to sort them into just their colors. Work together to do this as you talk about favorite colors, least favorite colors and make predictions about which color will have the most in its cup.

Make it easier -> use larger beads/ pieces of paper and fewer colors.

Make it harder -> after sorting, count each color and declare a winner.

CEREAL BRACELET

It's a craft you can eat!

You will need some chenille stems and circle cereal like Cheerios or Froot Loops. In my preschool classroom only about half of the students who chose this activity at free time actually took bracelets home. Many were more of a mid morning snack. That's OK because children are working on fine motor skills while picking the cereal up and while beading it on to the chenille stem.

Make it easier -> Add cereal on one end while they add it to the other. Teamwork makes everything easier!

Make it harder -> Using circle cereal that are multi-colored introduce the idea of patterns. "Pink, blue, pink, blue... what's next? "

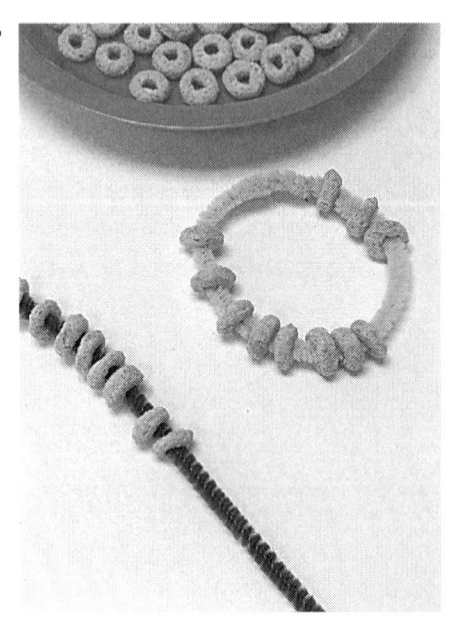

PLAYDOUGH CUTTING

This activity is a simple way to give your child the confidence to build scissor skills. Cutting paper can be tricky for beginners, so a better way to develop these skills is playdough. You can use kid scissors or all plastic scissors too.

Work the playdough into short snakes and then squish them so they are flat and start cutting. Remember to have your thumbs up while cutting.

FINE MOTOR ACTIVITIES

EGG & ORANGE PEELING

Get your preschoolers working on fine motor skills with these very practical kitchen tasks. Peeling hard-boiled eggs and mandarin oranges are wonderfully challenging tasks for little fingers.

Make it easier -> Help your child by doing a little bit of the peeling before handing the egg or orange off to them.

DOT STICKER BUGS

You can find these dot stickers in any drug store stationery aisle and every bog box store. They are cheap and a great tool to build fine motor skills. Of course, you can give your child a stack of them and let them create, but this is a great idea if you have a child looking for a little prompt.

Make sticker bugs. All you need is some paper, the dot stickers, and some crayons or colored pencils.

Make it easier -> Go up one size for the stickers making it easier for little fingers to peel and place.

Make it harder -> Ask your child to name the bug and write the name on the back of the paper.

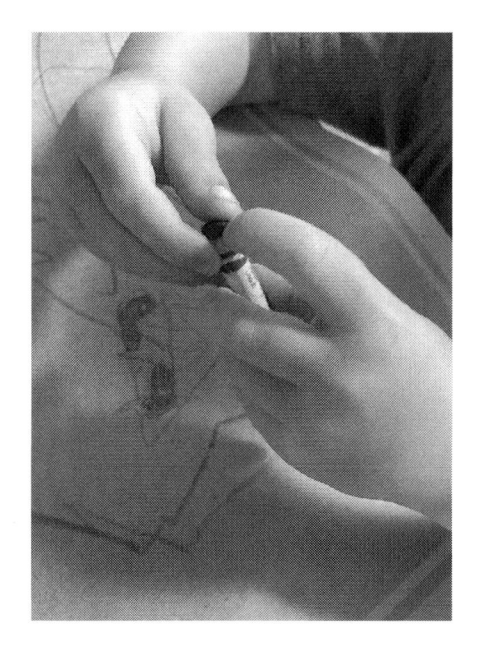

CRAYON PAPER PEELING

One of my goals for this book is to ensure that most of the activities are done with supplies you already have at home. This activity definitely hits that goal.

Peeling the paper off crayons is an incredible workout for little fingers. After the paper is off, show your child how to make big beautiful rubbings with the crayons.

FINE MOTOR ACTIVITIES

LEGO CHALLENGES

You will need some small Lego and an ice cube tray or dish. Dig through your child's Lego bin and find multiple pairs of identical bricks. Two red squares, two yellow rectangles, etc., use one brick from these pairs to make a simple creation. Next, leave the other set of bricks loose. Invite your child to use the loose bricks to replicate the bricks that are built. This activity not only works on fine motor skills but also on spatial and visual discrimination skills.

Make it easier -> Have two to three Lego challenges that are simple to recreate.

Make it harder -> Make six harder to replicate creations.

STICKER SHAPES

Stickers are one of the best fine motor materials out there, and they are so accessible!

This activity is exactly what it sounds like. Get some paper and draw a simple shape or a letter. If your child wants to draw the shape /letter all the better, but don't push. Now pop the stickers, whatever you have on hand, along with the shape. That's it!

Make it easier -> Keep the shape small and use larger stickers.

Make it harder -> Make the shape larger and use smaller stickers!

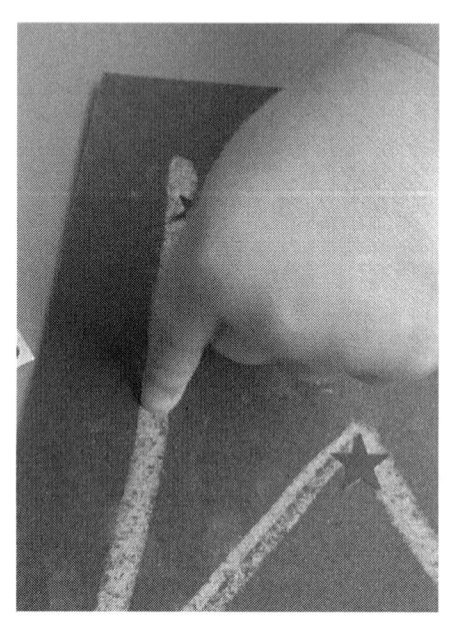

UNWRAP THE CORK (OR CAN)

Wrap multiple elastic bands around a wine cork or soup can. Invite your child to come "FREE" the cork or can from the elastic bands. This activity is so simple, but it's a challenge children enjoy.

Make it easier -> Use soup cans and only wrap the elastic around it once.
Make it harder-> Use wine corks and wrap the elastics around the cork multiple times.

FINE MOTOR ACTIVITIES

NATURE CUTTING

On a sunny day, find some kid scissors and head outside! Find all kinds of things you can cut: grass, flower petals, leaves. Remember to help your child hold the scissors correctly, with the wrist turned naturally and thumb up.

Make it easier -> This is so simple. There is no need to make it more so.

Make it harder -> If your child is starting to master scissors, ask them to cut you a specific shape from a large leaf!

*goggles are completely optional, though stylish.

SEQUIN LETTERS

Find some sturdy paper(recycled cereal boxes are great), white glue, and sequins. If you don't have sequins laying around, NO PROBLEM, just cut some colored paper into tiny squares. Next, you will want to write a letter on paper using a pencil. Hand your child the glue bottle and ask them to trace the letter with glue. Next, add the sequins or paper bits. Let dry.

Make it easier -> Keep the letter small and use larger sequins.

Make it harder -> Make the letter larger and use smaller sequins.

GLUE TRACING

Squeezing a bottle of white glue and tracing a shape sounds incredibly dull, but trust me, it's not, and preschoolers totally dig it.

You will need a bottle of white glue for this activity. You will also need a piece of sturdy paper and a marker. Draw lines, shapes, letters, whatever you want on the paper. Hand your child the glue and challenge them to trace the shapes. That's it. So simple, but this little activity helps develop several essential skills.

Make it easier -Make one or two simple shapes or letters like an X and an O.

Make it harder-> Write out sight words or their name to trace.

FINE MOTOR ACTIVITIES

RIPPED PAPER COLLAGE

This is a fun way to use the junk newspapers and other junk mail that usually go straight to the recycling bin. Ripping paper is a wonderful exercise of hand strength and fine motor skills. Gather some scrap paper and cut it into strips. After you have a large pile of ripped pieces, find a full sheet of paper and some glue to turn the collection of ripped pieces into art!

Make it easier -> Make small rips along the strips of paper to help your child start tearing the paper.

Make it harder -> No need to make this exercise harder.

BEADING WITH CANDY

This might not be your go-to fine motor activity, but it's a fun special day activity that gives your little one great fine motor practice. You will need some beading thread, you can use a chenille stem, but the plastic thread is better. Twizzlers work the best, but any candy with a hole will work. If you are using Twizzlers, you will want to cut them into beads first. Cut the thread you are using to the correct length and tape one end down on your table. This helps stop any accidental spills. Bead! When the beads are all on, tie it off and wear it proudly.

Make it easier -> Make a bracelet!

Make it harder -> Make a pattern with the candy.

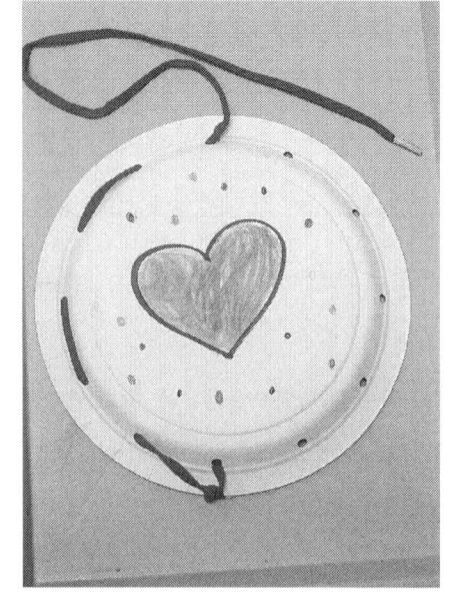

DIY LACING CARD

I include printable lacing cards in many of my thematic units, but my whole goal for this book is to use more available materials and make it so parents don't have to print anything out. This is a perfect example of that. This super simple lacing card is just a paper plate with holes punched along the edges. And a shoelace tied to it. You can decorate the plate you want and find a fun-colored shoelace, but that's extra, not needed at all. This simple activity works wonders for hand-eye coordination and, of course, fine motor skills.

Make it easier -> Use a dessert size plate.

Make it harder -> Number the holes so your child must go in a specific order while lacing.

GROSS MOTOR ACTIVITIES

Gross motor activities are crucial for development as well as children's overall health and wellness. Don't forget to move!

GROSS MOTOR

PAINTER'S TAPE BALANCE BEAM

Painter's tape is on my basic supply list for a reason; it's so versatile. For this activity, you will use it to make a balance beam on the floor. You can make it simple or use the tape to make a whole path for your child to balance around your home.

Make it more complex -> If this is too simple, add some pieces of paper with letters, shapes, or numbers for your child to identify along the way!

NATURE WALK

Fresh air is a must, even if it's just a short walk outside. What makes a nature walk different is that you will be stopping with your child and taking note of what's happening around you.

Listen, can you hear any animals or the wind? What's the weather? Are there any clouds in exciting shapes? Can you smell any flowers? What creatures do you see? Are there leaves on the trees?

Don't discount how important this activity is just because it's simple. Learning to observe the world around us is an important skill, and appreciating nature is something we too often overlook.

HIDE AND SEEK

Perfect for a day when the weather won't let you get outside this classic game is a great choice and yes, friends it's educational.

If you don't know how to play, here are the basics. One person sits at "home base" and counts (see math) to 30 while the other people hide. After that, they yell READY OR NOT HERE I COME and start searching for the hidden friends. When they find the people, those who have been found are out. Repeat.

When you play this with preschoolers, make sure to create ground rules about where you can and can not hide. Make sure any unsafe places like dryers, are inaccessible.

GROSS MOTOR

RHYME TAG

Get your child moving and rhyming with this fun game. Before you play, make sure that your child can identify and rhyme words pretty fluently.
The game is simple and a lot like freeze tag. When you were tagged, you have to freeze and wait for someone to crawl under your legs to unfreeze you. In this version of the game, the unfreezer calls out a word, and the frozen player must yell out a word that rhymes with it to get back into the game.

This is a fun game to play with a mixed age group, but you can play with just two players. In that case, the person who is "it" tags the other player, and they must freeze. The person who is "it" yells out a word, and the frozen player must respond with a rhyme to be unfrozen; now, they are "it."

ALPHABET TOSS

Grab a soft ball, some bean bags, or roll some socks together to make your own. You will also need some paper (any old paper will do) and a marker. Write one letter on each piece of paper. I like to do three pieces of paper and write two familiar letters and one that your child hasn't mastered yet.
When it's time to play, stand your child a few feet from the paper and hand them the ball or bean bag. Call out a letter and have them toss the ball to that target. Keep going!

Make it easier-> Use colored paper and write the same letter on every sheet. Call out the color and letter together " Toss the ball to the yellow a.' this will reinforce letter recognition while using the color, which your child already knows as the differentiating factor.

Make it harder --> Use sight words! There is a list of sight words in the appendix.

SIDEWALK CHALK LETTER STOMP

Grab some sidewalk chalk and head outside. Write letters on the ground and invite your child to play. Call out a letter and have your child run to it and stomp on the letter, repeat!

You don't have to limit yourself to letters for this activity, you can use shapes, numbers, or if your child is ready, sight words too.
On a hot day, grab the hose or squirt guns and spray the chalk letters instead of stomping.

GROSS MOTOR

LAUNDRY BASKETBALL

This activity is straightforward, a toss game that uses socks and laundry baskets to get your wiggles out. Gather a few laundry baskets and some soft balls or socks rolled into balls. If you want, you can grab some painter's tape and make a free throw line on your floor. Now it's time to toss and get some baskets!

Make it more complex -> Add some numbers to each laundry basket and assign points for every successful throw. Keep a tally and add it up at the end or compete against each other.

HEAD, SHOULDERS, KNEES AND TOES

You remember this song, right?

*Head, shoulders, knees, and toes.
Knees and toes.
Head, shoulders, knees, and toes.
Knees and toes.
Eyes and ears, mouth, and nose.
Head, shoulders, knees, and toes.
Knees and toes!*

Sing it while touching each body part. Sing it fast, sing it very, very slow.

ANIMAL MOVES

Mix gross motor, a little science, and a lot of pretend play together for this activity. All you need to do is find a spot with lots of room. Inside with the couch pushed aside or outside on the grass if you have a yard.

Call out an animal and have your child move all around like that animal. Call out another and see what your child's imagination and knowledge about that animal combine to create.

Some of my favorite animals to call out?
The sky's the limit, but I like to call out frog, snake, monkey, snail, tiger, butterfly, grasshopper, elephant, dolphin, etc.

GROSS MOTOR

NATURE COLOR HUNT

Run around outside and find colors while getting some much needed outdoor time. Yell out a color and have your child run to find it.

Repeat.

So simple but so good for their brains and bodies!

TOY CAR WASH

Wash your bikes, ride-on toys, and cozy coupes with real sponges, and if you are brave, hand your child the hose. You will want to do this on a warm day, but it's so much fun and functional too.

BUILD A FORT

Building a fort isn't just about gross motor development; though it does work on that, it also taps into STEM learning. STEM stands for Science, Technology, Engineering, and Math, and fort building fits this category. There is as much problem solving while building a fort as lifting, carrying, and pushing couches out of the way.

After you build it, grab some books and read them together!

SOCIAL & EMOTIONAL

These activities are some you can use at home to work on developing stronger social and emotional skills. Pretend play is a wonderful vehicle to work on these skills.

SOCIAL & EMOTIONAL

MIRROR MIRROR

Children develop empathy in different ways as they grow, but for us to be able to talk to them effectively about emotions, they have to recognize and name them. This activity is a fun way to work on that.

Sit facing your child and tell them that you are going to be each other's magic mirror. You will take turns saying "Mirror, mirror, on the wall who's the (insert emotion) of them all? And then you each have to make a face with that emotion.

Try angry, happy, sad, frustrated, bored, scared, silly, and any other you can think of.

RED LIGHT, GREEN LIGHT

You might think of this game as one played at recess, but it's a wonderful way to help your child develop impulse control and work on listening skills. These are vital for social, emotional development.
If you have never played before, here are the basic rules. Go somewhere where you can run. The caller stands away from the group (or single child) and calls out green light - green means go, so the children walk or run towards the caller. If they yell out yellow, you must slow down, and red means stop immediately.

Yell out the three colors in random order until your child has reached you and then switch places. Letting your child be the caller gives them a chance to be in control, which is essential, especially during a crisis.

IF YOU'RE HAPPY & YOU KNOW IT

This classic song is one of my favorite ways to talk to children about emotions. Instead of singing the classic lyrics, replace happy in subsequent verses with different emotions:

Mad – cross your arms.
Frustrated – stomp your feet.
Excited – jump up and down.
Sad – make a frown
Scared – hide your face.

As you sing the song, ask your child to mimic your facial expressions and guess what emotion you are showing them.

The lyrics can be found in the appendix.

SOCIAL & EMOTIONAL

HOW DO THEY FEEL?

Young children are still learning to differentiate emotions during their preschool years, and sometimes they aren't sure how their friends feel. Having the correct words and practicing reading other's feelings helps children develop and practice empathy.

For this activity, you can use family photos of people expressing different emotions. If you only have happy pictures, follow the link in the appendix for free printable images.

Go through the pictures with your child, ask them how the people feel. Why do they feel this way? Listen to their explanation. Many young children associate crying with physical pain and not emotional. If this is the case, it's not wrong, but offer your suggestions too.

TEA PARTY

Listening and having conversations are essential skills for social, emotional development. When we listen to each other, we are working on connecting and nurturing relationships. Having a tea party is a great way to help these skills develop.
Gather some fancy cups, a teapot or lovely juice jug, some cookies or fruit, and chat during a break in your workday. Model active listening, ask open-ended questions, and set a place for a favorite stuffed friend or doll.

BIG BREATH BLOW PAINTING

When things get chaotic in my class or at home, I often say, " Let's take a big breath and blow it out." which works beautifully if a child knows how to do that. If they haven't practiced it, they will probably start breathing very quickly, which doesn't calm anyone.

Practice big breaths before this activity—big breaths in through your nose and out through your mouth.

Get some water, food color (or liquid watercolors if you have them), a straw, and paper. Add some colored water to your paper and then take a big breath and with the straw, slowly but firmly blow at the colored water, so it spreads. Repeat.

BEDTIME READING

Reading at bedtime is a great way to calm children before sleep; it's also a great way to make reading a part of your daily routine. These questions are a vital part of bedtime reading because they work to connect your child to the material while also working on foundational literacy skills.

Choose one or two questions to focus on nightly before, during, or after you read.

Before reading, ask your child what they think the book will be about. What do the pictures on the cover tell us?

While reading, ask your child to use the illustrations to give them clues to what each page will be about before reading it.

Ask your child to try to find their initials at least once in every book you read tonight. If this is too easy, try giving them a simple word to find like the or and.

While reading, stop and ask your child how they would feel in the character's shoes. Would they make the same choices? Would it be fun to be in the book?

After you read, ask your child if they could be one of the characters in the book who would it be and why?

After you are done reading a book, ask your child to tell you in their words what happened in the book. This skill is called retelling, and it is a necessary skill in reading comprehension.

After reading, ask your child to come up with an alternate ending to the story.

After reading, ask your child to think about a time when they felt the same way as one of the characters.

After reading, ask your child what title they would give the book if they could change the title.

After you read, ask your child what their favorite part of the book was. Why?

APPENDIX

MUST HAVE PRESCHOOL BOOKS

Alphabet Books
Animalia by Graham Base
Eating the Alphabet: Fruits & Vegetables from A to Z by Lois Ehlert
Alphabet Under Construction by Denise Fleming
Chicka Chicka Boom Boom: Anniversary Edition by Bill Martin Jr. and John Archambault
Learn The Alphabet with Northwest Coast Native Art
Pride Puppy by Robin Stevenson

Awesome Read Aloud Books
Whoever You Are by Mem Fox
Something From Nothing by Phoebe Gilman
Lovely by Jess Hong
Pete The Cat And His Four Groovy Buttons by Eric Litwin
Zoom! by Robert Munsch
If You Give a Mouse a Cookie by Laura Joffe Numeroff
I Love You Stinky Face by Lisa McCourt
Mortimer by Robert Munsch
Mary Had A Little Glam by Tammi Sauer
Where the Wild Things Are by Maurice Sendak
Press Here by Herve Tullet
Don't Let the Pigeon Drive the Bus! by Mo Willems
Jabari Jumps by Gaia Cornwall

Books About Colors
Rainbow Stew by Cathryn Falwell
Planting a Rainbow by Lois Elhert
Little Blue and Little Yellow by Leo Lionni
Brown Bear, Brown Bear, What Do You See? by Bill Martin Jr.
Pink Is For Boys by Robb Pearlman
A Gift for Amma by Meera Sriram
Mouse Paint by Ellen Stoll Walsh

Counting Books
Big Fat Hen by Keith Baker
Granny Went to Market by Stella Blackstone
Goodnight Moon 123 by Margaret Wise Brown
Fish Eyes: A Book You Can Count On by Lois Elhert
Mouse Count by Ellen Stoll Walsh

APPENDIX

MUST HAVE PRESCHOOL BOOKS

Books About Emotions & Self-Identity
I'll Wait, Mr. Panda by Steve Antony
I Am Enough by Grace Byers
The Way I Feel by Janan Cain
The Many Colors of Harpreet Singh by Supriya Kelkar
Keisha Ann Can! By Daniel Kirk
It's Mine! by Leo Lionni
Julian is A Mermaid by Jessica Love
Elmer by David McKee
Tough Guys Have Feelings Too by Keith Negley
Your Name Is A Song by Jamilah Thompkins-Bigelow
Owl Babies by Martin Waddell

Books About Food & Families
Everybody Cooks Rice by Nora Dooley
A Day With Yahyah by Julie Flett
Fry Bread by Kevin Noble Maillard
Everywhere Babies by Susan Meyers and Marla Frazee
A Family is a Family is a Family by Sara O'Leary
The Family Book by Todd Parr
Sam is My Sister by Ashley Rhodes-Courter
Bilal Cooks Daal by Aisha Saeed
Pizza at Sally's by Monica Wellington

Rhyming Books
(many other books included in other sections also rhyme)
I Ain't Gonna Paint No More! by Karen Beaumont
How Big Is a Pig? by Claire Beaton
My Truck is Stuck! by Kevin Lewis
One Duck Stuck by Phyllis Root

Shape Books
City Shapes by Diana Murray
My Heart Is Like a Zoo by Michael Hall
Perfect Square by Michael Hall
Mouse Shapes by Ellen Stoll Walsh

APPENDIX

MUST HAVE PRESCHOOL BOOKS

Thematic Books
There are so many more books but these are my favorites. Find hundreds of book lists on my site **notimeforflashcards.com**

Not Norman! by Kelly Bennet (Pets/ Friendship)

Penguinaut by Marcie Colleen (Space)

On the LaunchPad: A Counting Book About Rockets by Michael Dahl (Space/counting)

Dinosaurs, Dinosaurs by Byron Barton (Dinosaurs)

The Mitten by Jan Brett (Winter)

Big Red Barn by Margaret Wise Brown (Farm)

A House for Hermit Crab by Eric Carle (Sealife/months of the year)

The Very Hungry Caterpillar by Eric Carle (Days of the week, nutrition, bugs)

Monster Trouble by Lane Fredrickson (Monsters)

Is Your Mama a Llama? by Deborah Guarino (Animals/families)

The Night Flower by Laura Hawthorne (Desert habitat)

The Snowy Day by Ezra Jack Keats (Weather/winter)

Dig Dig Digging by Margaret Mayo (Transportation)

Lola at the Library by Anna McQuinn (Reading)

Lola Gets A Cat by Anna McQuinn (Pets)

Lola Plants A Garden by Anna McQuinn (Garden)

From Tadpole to Frog by Wendy Pfeffer (Spring/pond life/life cycles)

Our Stars by Anne Rockwell (Space)

Dinosaur Roar! Board Book by Paul and Henrietta Stickland (Dinosaurs/opposites)

Leaves by David Ezra Stein (Seasons/hibernation)

I Love Bugs! by Philemon Sturges (Bugs)

Firefighter Frank by Monica Wellington (Fire safety/community helpers)

Big Earth, Little Me by Thom Wiley (Earth day/nature)

Poles Apart by Jeanne Willis (Polar animals/ travel)

Trashy Town by Andrea Zimmerman and David Clemesha (Community helpers)

APPENDIX

BASIC SUPPLIES

Multi-color pack of construction paper
Plain white paper
Crayons
Markers
Glue (bottle of white glue)
Pencils
Paint
Watercolors
Paintbrushes
Kid scissors
Chenille stems (pipe cleaners)
Painter's tape
Dice

PLAYDOUGH RECIPE

Ingredients:

2 1/2 cups all-purpose flour
1/2 cup salt
3 Tablespoons oil
1 tablespoon alum or 3 tablespoon cream of tartar
2 cups boiling water
food coloring of your choice

Mix all ingredients together in a heatproof bowl.
If it's too sticky, add a little extra oil.
If it's too oily, I add a little extra flour.
Too much flour makes it dry out fast

APPENDIX

SIGHT WORD LIST

Most preschoolers will not be ready for sight words. Please do not worry about using this list unless your child has mastered letter recognition, matching upper and lowercase letters, and has a real desire to start sounding out words. Most sight words can be sounded out (decoded), so do not ignore this step when introducing them. Use this list as a resource for which words to use for the games in the book if letters no longer pose a challenge. There is NO rush. I have included this list as an extra for differentiation, not an expectation.

a	funny	look	see
and	go	make	the
away	help	me	three
big	here	my	to
blue	I	not	two
can	in	one	up
come	is	play	we
down	it	red	where
find	jump	run	yellow
for	little	said	you

LINKS TO ADDITIONAL RESOURCES

FREE Resources

Roll & Cover Game Boards
https://www.notimeforflashcards.com/wp-content/uploads/2020/04/roll-and-cover-game-boards.pdf

Swim, Fly or Walk Sorting Cards
https://www.notimeforflashcards.com/wp-content/uploads/2020/07/swim-fly-walk.pdf

Emotions Cards
https://www.notimeforflashcards.com/wp-content/uploads/2016/05/sad-or-mad-photos-.pdf

More FREE learning at home resources for when you have more time or just need some new ideas!
https://www.notimeforflashcards.com/learning-at-home-during-coronavirus

Book Lists for Preschool
https://www.notimeforflashcards.com/category/book-list

Resources for sale

Rhyming Blocks
https://www.notimeforflashcards.com/2021/04/rhyming-blocks-printable.html

Letter Sound Cards
https://www.notimeforflashcards.com/2021/07/letter-sound-sorting-cards.html

APPENDIX

SONGS AND FINGERPLAYS

The Weather Song
The song is sung to the tune of "Clementine" and use the following actions as you sing:
What's the weather? (Arms out like you are asking a question)
What's the weather? (Arms out like you are asking a question)
What's the weather everyone? (Arms out like you are asking a question)
Is it windy? (Sway arms back and forth)
Is it cloudy? (Wiggle palms making clouds in the air)
Is there rain? (Make rain with fingers)
Or is there sun? (Make a circle with two hands and raise it above your head)

The Wheels On The Bus
The wheels on the bus go round and round, round and round, round and round.
The wheels on the bus go round and round, all through the town!

The driver on the bus goes move on back, move on back, move on back.
The driver on the bus goes move on back, all through the town!

The money on the bus goes clink clink clink, clink clink clink, clink clink clink.
The money on the bus goes clink clink clink, all through the town!

The people on the bus go up and down, up and down, up and down.
The people on the bus go up and down, all through the town!

The babies on the bus go waa waa waa, waa waa waa, waa waa waa!
The babies on the bus go waa waa waa, all through the town!

The wipers on the bus go swish swish swish, swish swish swish, swish swish swish.
The wipers on the bus go swish swish swish, all through the town!

APPENDIX

SONGS AND FINGERPLAYS

Five Little Ducks
Five little ducks went out to play,
over the hills and far away.
Mother duck said" Quack quack quack quack!"
but only four little ducks came back!

Continues 4, 3, 2, 1 and ends with " And 5 little ducks came waddling back!"

Five Little Monkeys
Five little monkeys swinging in a tree.
Along came a crocodile as sneaky as can be.
One little monkey said "Betcha can't catch me!" (Stick your tongue out).
SNAP (Clap hands together).

Repeat for 4, 3, 2.

One Little Monkey swinging in a tree.
Along came a crocodile as sneaky as can be.
One little monkey said" Betcha can't catch me! (stick tongue out)
"SNAP!" (clap hands together).
"Nah Nah you missed me!" (stick tongue out).

Five Little Frogs
Five Little frogs sitting on a well, (Have five fingers on one hand out)
One looked in and down he fell. (Hold one finger up, then point him down to the ground and fall)
Frogs jumped high! (Jump up and hold both hands up overhead)
Frogs jumped low! (Crouch down and hold both hands down to the ground)
Frogs jumped everywhere, to and fro! (Jump all around and move arms all around)

You can continue with 4, 3, 2, 1 frogs if you if want or just do one verse.

APPENDIX

SONGS AND FINGERPLAYS

Blast Off
Climb aboard the spaceship (climb up a ladder with your arms)
we're going to the moon (point to the moon in the sky).
Hurry and get ready (pump arms like you are running)
we're going to blast off soon (keep pumping arms).
Put on your helmet, (pop on an imaginary helmet)
and buckle up real tight (buckle up, I usually do 3 or 4 buckles).
Cause here comes the countdown(take a deep breath),
so count with all your might!
10, 9, 8, 7, 6, 5, 4, 3, 2, 1,(use your hands to count)
Blast Off!(raise and shake hands in the air)

Little Fishy
To The Tune Of "I'm A Little Teapot"
I'm a little fishy watch me go.
I swim fast, and I swim slow.
When the sharks come out, I dare not play.
I dive down deep and swim away!

Shake Your Sillies Out
Shake shake shake your sillies out!
Shake shake shake your sillies out!
Shake shake shake your sillies out,
and wiggle all your worries away!

Flick flick flick your fidgets out!
Flick flick flick your fidgets out!
Flick flick flick your fidgets out,
and wiggle all your worries away!

Jump jump jump your jiggles out!
Jump jump jump your jiggles out!
Jump jump jump your jiggles out,
and wiggle all your worries away!

APPENDIX

NURSERY RHYMES

Twinkle Twinkle Little Star
Twinkle, twinkle, little star, how I wonder what you are.
Up above the world so high, like a diamond in the sky.
Twinkle, twinkle, little star, how I wonder what you are.

The Itsy Bitsy Spider
The itsy bitsy spider crawled up the water spout.
Down came the rain, and washed the spider out.
Out came the sun, and dried up all the rain, and the itsy bitsy spider went up the spout again

Hickory Dickory Dock
Hickory, dickory, dock, The mouse ran up the clock.
The clock struck one.
The mouse ran down.
Hickory, dickory, dock.

Jack and Jill
Jack and Jill went up the hill,
to fetch a pail of water.
Jack fell down,
and broke his crown.
And Jill came tumbling after.

Humpty Dumpty
Humpty Dumpty sat on a wall.
Humpty Dumpty had a great fall.
All the king's horses and all the king's men,
couldn't put Humpty together again.

Hey Diddle Diddle
Hey, diddle, diddle.
The cat and the fiddle,
the cow jumped over the moon;
The little dog laughed
To see such sport.
And the dish ran away with the spoon.

ABOUT THE AUTHOR

Allison McDonald B.A., B.Ed, M.S

Hi again.

I hope you've found this book useful. I have two other books published by Scholastic if you want to check them out; **Raising A Rock-Star Reader** is for families and caregivers, while **Setting The Stage for Rock-Star Readers** is for classroom early childhood educators. You can find them at the Scholastic Store and anywhere else books are sold online.

For decades, I have been teaching preschoolers - taking a few breaks to have my own children and start my blog **notimeforflashcards.com.**

I have two bachelor's degrees, the first in Canadian history (not so relevant, but I'm good at Jeopardy) and the second in elementary education focused on early literacy. My master's degree is in early childhood and family development. I am currently looking at doctorate programs because I don't feel like I am done with school learning just yet.

I'm not sure what the 2021-2022 school year will look like. I hope I'll get to teach in person all year. Like many of you, uncertainty is the only constant right now. I do hope that this book is one tool you have to ease some uncertainty. No matter what you know, you have simple ways to teach your child at home.

You can do this even if you never planned to.

© 2021. ALL RIGHTS RESERVED. FILES ARE FOR NON- COMMERCIAL USE. PERSONAL AND CLASSROOM USE ONLY. DO NOT MODIFY, DUPLICATE FOR DISTRIBUTION, SELL OR REDISTRIBUTE.

Printed in Great Britain
by Amazon